This is D. A. at his best—gospel-rich, raw, in tune with culture, and deeply insightful regarding human nature. Written by one of this generation's most capable communicators, these pages describe a struggle that consumes most of us, and they highlight a simple yet profound path of redemption—faith in God's grace.

J. D. GREEAR, PHD
Author, *Gaining by Losing: Why the Future Belongs to Churches that Send* and *Jesus, Continued . . . : Why the Spirit inside You Is Better than Jesus beside You*

The opening pages of this book are gut wrenching, the story of a boy who learns he can never live up to the expectations of his dad. But what follows is exhilarating, liberating, and life giving. D. A. Horton is one of my favorite young leaders in evangelicalism, and this book will show you why. If you have ever struggled, as I perpetually do, with the temptation to believe that God is pleased with you on the basis of your performance, this is the book you need to read. With pastoral wisdom and sharp focus, D. A. Horton shows us how to rest in the most radical pronouncement that could ever be made of us: "You are my beloved son, and in you I am well pleased."

RUSSELL MOORE
President, Southern Baptist Ethics & Religious Liberty Commission

The truth of God's Word sets peopl~ ~ ~~~ ~ap. D. A. walks us through his st~~ ~~~ ~~~~ ~ set him free. May we follow hi~ ~~~ ~~~ ~ in Christ.

O. RAY HORTO~
Father of D. A. H~

D. A. Horton is brilliant! He's a gift to the church. As you read the beautifully and powerfully written *Bound to Be Free*, you will see why. In the midst of a performance-based culture where people are exhausted, D. A. invites us to come and rest in the performance of Jesus. Paradoxically, as we rest in Jesus' performance, Jesus lives out his glorification of God through us. You are going to love this book. Your life will be transformed.

DR. DERWIN L. GRAY
Author of *The High Definition Leader: Building Multiethnic Churches in a Multiethnic World*

Many today live enslaved to achievement and to the demand to impress others, and they burn themselves out in the process. Horton offers another path which offers true freedom and life to the full.

MICHAEL HIDALGO
Author of *Changing Faith: Questions, Doubts and Choices about an Unchanging God*

A life in ministry is hard, and while we serve God, we often find ourselves trapped in service to other motivations that lead us away from God's life-giving grace. In *Bound to Be Free*, D. A. Horton presents us with a transparent and compelling case for the liberation that comes only when we bind ourselves to the cross of Christ. This book will be an encouragement, especially to pastors and church planters.

ED STETZER
President of Lifeway Research, www.edstetzer.com

Escaping Performance

BOUND TO BE FREE

to Be Captured by Grace

D. A. HORTON

A NavPress resource published in alliance
with Tyndale House Publishers, Inc.

NavPress is the publishing ministry of The Navigators, an international Christian organization and leader in personal spiritual development. NavPress is committed to helping people grow spiritually and enjoy lives of meaning and hope through personal and group resources that are biblically rooted, culturally relevant, and highly practical.

For more information, visit www.NavPress.com.

Bound to Be Free: Escaping Performance to Be Captured by Grace

Copyright © 2016 by D. A. Horton. All rights reserved.

A NavPress resource published in alliance with Tyndale House Publishers, Inc.

NAVPRESS and the NAVPRESS logo are registered trademarks of NavPress, The Navigators, Colorado Springs, CO. *TYNDALE* is a registered trademark of Tyndale House Publishers, Inc. Absence of ® in connection with marks of NavPress or other parties does not indicate an absence of registration of those marks.

Cover design by Stephen Vosloo
Cover photograph courtesy Björn Simon/Unsplash.com.
Author photo taken by Matt Engelking, copyright © 2015. All rights reserved.

The Team:
Don Pape, Publisher
Caitlyn Carlson, Acquisitions Editor

Published in association with the literary agency of Wolgemuth & Associates, Inc.

Library of Congress Cataloging-in-Publication Data

Names: Horton, D. A.
Title: Bound to be free : escaping performance to be captured by grace / D. A. Horton.
Description: Colorado Springs : NavPress, 2016. | Includes bibliographical references.
Identifiers: LCCN 2015033533 | ISBN 9781631464676
Subjects: LCSH: Liberty—Religious aspects—Christianity. | Grace (Theology) | Performance—Religious aspects—Christianity.
Classification: LCC BT810.3 .H67 2016 | DDC 248.4—dc23
LC record available at http://lccn.loc.gov/2015033533

Printed in the United States of America

22	21	20	19	18	17	16
7	6	5	4	3	2	1

CONTENTS

ACKNOWLEDGMENTS

To:

God the Father who unconditionally loves me. God the Son who saved me, is saving me, and will save me. God the Holy Spirit who lives in me, providing me with strength to mature spiritually.

Elicia, Izabelle, Lola, and Duce. Being free in Christ allows me to savor every moment I spend with you. You all *are* my first ministry. I'm so blessed to have you all in my life.

Ray and Rita Horton. Thank you for loving me at all times, Mom and Dad.

The elders and members of Koinonia Bible Church. Thank you for allowing me the grace to serve alongside you all.

Dhati Lewis, Kevin Ezell, Lecrae, Matt Letourneau, Nehemiah Weaver, and John O. Thank you for shepherding my heart. I'm privileged to call you brothers and friends.

Andrew Wolgemuth. Thank you for being more than an agent but also a friend.

Don Pape and Caitlyn Carlson. Thank you for helping me capture quality content and for shaping it to encourage believers everywhere.

INTRODUCTION

Growing up, I believed that if I didn't win all of my wrestling matches, if I wasn't perfect, my dad wouldn't want me anymore.

You see, before every tournament, my dad would give me a rundown of my competitors, tell me how I could beat them, and remind me that if I lost, he would be disappointed. Tournament after tournament and year after year I experienced one of two realities. If I won, I would have my dad's affection. If I lost, he would withdraw emotionally, and the ride home, no matter the length, would be filled with intimidating silence.

When I was thirteen, I decided I wanted to face my biggest fear head-on to see how my dad would respond if I purposefully didn't aim for perfection. My experiment couldn't have taken place in a more climactic environment: the state tournament.

I entered the tournament as the top seed and was picked to win my fifth state title. After breezing through the first round of competition, I entered the quarterfinals certain that I could beat my opponent—but focused more on putting on a show for all the people who crowded around the mat than on the match itself. I was, as my dad would say, *horsing around*. My plan was to remain in control of the entire match and earn a semifinal bid by scoring a takedown in the closing seconds of the third and final period. I had it all worked out.

Things were going according to plan until the unthinkable happened. As I tried to take my opponent down in the third period, he countered and quickly caught me as I slipped. The buzzer sounded, and the referee held up two points for my opponent. I had lost the match. But I wasn't disappointed— losing was just another way to get back at my dad after years of riding an emotional roller coaster.

I watched the referee raise my opponent's hand as he was declared the victor. As I nonchalantly smiled and shook his hand, he said, "Thank you," as if he knew I had not tried my best. I gave him a hug and told him that he was sure to be the next state champion.

As I walked off the mat toward the corner where my dad and coaches had sat just moments before, I noticed my clothes sitting on the floor in a pile.

My dad was nowhere to be found.

At first, I figured he had stepped outside the arena to have a cigarette, a Coke, and a conversation with himself about my poor performance in order to cool down. I took the pocket change I had in my bag and grabbed some lunch before deciding to take a nap. When I woke up, most of my teammates had already gone back to our hotel. Suddenly nervous, I walked around the arena, looking at thousands of faces—but none of them was my dad's.

There's no way my dad left me here alone and drove back home to Kansas City, I told myself. We lived hours away. He wouldn't really leave me.

Hours passed as I searched and searched. You have to remember, this was before the era of cell phones, so it's not as if I could've texted or FaceTimed my dad. Finally, I asked one of my coaches for some change so I could call my older brother, who was back in Kansas City. My coach asked if I was okay, and of course pride kept me from confessing my fear that my dad had abandoned me. As I picked up the phone, my hand shook, and an overwhelming sense of panic overtook me.

I fought back the tears, my mouth trembling. When my brother answered the phone, my emotional dam burst. He was trying to make sense of what I was saying, asking me to calm down and explain what was going on. Finally I yelled out, "He left me! I'm here at the state tournament all by myself! He left me, Raymond—he really left me!" My brother, thinking the best of our dad, began to interrogate me about what I had done to make our dad so angry that I'd think he might leave me at the state tournament. Embarrassed, I confessed that I hadn't tried my best and had lost the quarterfinal match. My brother, still not believing my story, told me to go with one of my coaches back to the hotel and wait to hear from him.

Right after he got off the phone with me, he called our mom and dad's house. Within two rings, he was greeted by my dad's voice. I still don't know what words they exchanged that day, which I think is for the best. Later that night, my brother met me at the hotel, checked into a room with his wife and daughter, and had me stay with them. Before we went to bed, he challenged me to forget about all that had taken place and to focus on the work I had to do to finish the tournament well.

The next morning I woke up feeling nauseated. I wasn't worried about my performance or even walking away with a state plaque. I was afraid of facing my dad after the tournament was over. A myriad of questions ran through my mind the rest of the day. My emotions swung like a pendulum between anger and guilt. I thought I would feel this way for the rest of my life.

My brother showed me how to use my emotions as fuel to drive me in my competition that day. I breezed through my first three matches and entered into the consolation finals, facing an opponent that I beat the week before in the district championship. Right before the match, my brother and I prayed together. Then he looked me in the eye and asked me if I was ready. By this time I was completely spent. I told him I wanted to go home. He just smiled, gave me a hug, and told me, as he did before every match, that he was in my corner. "Do your best, *mijo.*"

I lost the match 5 to 1 and received the fourth-place plaque for my age and weight division. As my brother and his wife drove me home, they counseled me on how to forgive my dad for what he had done and told me not to agitate him to the point of physical confrontation. I knew things would be okay when I got home because my dad, who worked the overnight shift, was probably at work.

The next morning I woke up for school, knowing that I had to be out of the house before my dad normally arrived home at 6:30 a.m. I got ready in record time, unpacked my wrestling bag, set my fourth-place plaque on the dining-room table, and walked out the door to my bus stop. Throughout the course of the day I felt a tug of war within my heart. I knew I had to eventually face my dad, and I didn't know what to say or how I would respond. In those days, I tried to avoid conflict at all costs—I remember praying I'd meet with some tragedy like getting shot or jumped so he would extend me compassion instead of wrath.

The bus ride home that day was filled with the typical inner-city middle school aura: objects thrown, insults hurled at the bus driver, and threats of gang violence among rivals. In the midst of this chaos, I felt like I was in the eye of the storm, calmly awaiting the destruction that lay ahead. When I got off at my bus stop at the corner of 18th Street and Washington, my one-block walk home felt more like the Green Mile. I gave departing handshakes to the homies before looking up at my house, consumed by fear. Then I took a breath and walked up the stairs.

My dad was still asleep as he normally was when I came home from school. I knew he wouldn't wake up until around seven that evening to get ready for work. I had a few hours of peace to figure out if I was going to stay in the house or go hang out with my friends. As I approached the kitchen to get a snack, I looked at the dining room table and saw my plaque.

The word *LOSER* was engraved four times all over it.

My fear morphed into blood-boiling rage. I looked at that plaque in utter disbelief. This couldn't be real life. Seized by anger and hurt, I decided at that moment never to let my dad have a hand up on me emotionally, mentally, or physically ever again. Never again would I give my dad entrance into my life, I swore. Not only had he abandoned me, he also had destroyed my plaque, which showed me once and for all that nothing I ever did would be good enough for him.

So why am I telling you this story? Because the way I saw my dad while growing up is the way a lot of us look at God. We can feel like He'll only affirm us, stay close to us, and acknowledge us if we constantly push ourselves toward perfection in our performance for Him. One definition of *performance* is "an action, task, or operation, seen in terms of how successfully it was performed."[1] And we can think that if we're successful in our performance for God, He'll be happy with us.

Up until two years ago, I was in a perpetual state of burnout because I felt my endless performance was my reasonable service to God. Much like a shark has to stay in sync with the current of the ocean in order to breathe, I was sure that my life had to remain in constant motion for me to receive the attention and affirmation of God. The irony was that I allowed my *calling* to keep me divorced from resting in Jesus. I've been given the privilege by God to preach the gospel of grace, a truth centered on the work of Christ—and yet I felt the need to perform (work) in order to gain God's favor.

THE PERFORMANCE LIFE

I'm the type of person who, by design, is always on the go. My mom tells people that I began *running* when I was seven months old. You read that right—running, not walking! My teachers in grade school would pin notes on my shirt to tell my parents about the "ambitious" activities I performed in front of my class that day and how I would refuse to take my seat when asked. When I was five years old, my parents signed me up for wrestling, hoping it would serve as an outlet for all of my energy. As I grew older, my drive to "do something" never ran out of gas. I hated being still. That same high-energy level that was *cute* when I was young became a *curse* as I grew into adulthood.

Soon after my conversion to Christianity, I began laboring in the work of ministry. The thought behind this was, *I need to stay busy to stay out of the streets.* I'm wired in such a way that when I'm bored, I'm probably going to find something to keep me occupied—and whatever that *something* is, it's likely some form of mischief. So I joined as many ministries in the church as I could to keep off the streets of the hood that I was raised in.

I convinced myself during my initial days of salvation that busyness equaled holiness. If I was idle, I was sinning and God was mad at me. Couple this belief with the theological teaching that you can sin your way *out* of salvation, and the result is an explosive concoction that prompts many to turn their backs on the church, Christianity (at least the version they've been exposed to), and ultimately God Himself.

To say my life was packed beyond capacity would be an understatement. Day after day I would be the first to rise and the last to lie down (notice I didn't say sleep). Vacations? Nah, I never took them. Growing up poor, we could never afford one, so I learned to live without them—and just thinking about taking one day off, let alone seven, ushered the sin of anxiety onto the throne of my heart. I said yes to every conference I was asked to speak at, refused to delegate responsibilities to others who had a desire to help, and felt guilty asking any of the other church leaders for help because I was *paid* to pastor and they were not. I would regularly brush off the stern warning of "slow down" offered to me by my wife, employers, friends, and mentors. People would ask me when I found time to sleep, and my response would be, "I'll rest when I'm dead."

I felt like an entertainer spinning a series of plates on top of long and limber sticks, hoping to keep the plates spinning so they wouldn't fall and shatter on the stage below. I believed the lie that God had sentenced me to a life of performing for His love. I lived in constant fear that if at any moment one of the plates (family and ministry responsibilities) were to come crashing down, I would not only be at fault but would have to pay God back for the broken plate before buying a new one to start my routine all over again. Life was a never-ending performance for an audience of one who, according to my misguided heart, could at any moment leave the venue, heckling me and demanding a full refund.

The ugliest moment of this curse came during a phone call with my wife as I boarded a plane to Chicago to teach at a conference on healthy urban churches.

Elicia and I were arguing over my *being a resident but not present* at home. The core of her argument highlighted my zombie-like state of mind when I was at home, not on the road traveling or at work. During these times I lacked meaningful engagement with her and our two daughters. Elicia brought up this blind spot so much that I had grown inoculated to it. So when she started talking about it before I boarded the plane, I grew irritated beyond words. In this moment of frustration I chose to do what no husband should ever do: I interrupted Elicia mid-sentence and told her I needed to get off the phone. With a fearful tremble in her voice she uttered two words that still give me chills:

"I'm done."

When I asked her what she meant, she hung up the phone.

When Elicia said, "I'm done," she meant she couldn't keep up with the insane rhythm of life I was forcing on our entire family. Everything I was doing—working a full-time job, being a full-time seminary student, traveling to preach and perform gospel rap concerts, all while planting a church in the city—had run my marriage into the ground. At first I thought she was out of line, and immediately I pushed aside her feelings, rehearsing my cross-examination and rebuttal and deciding I would lay out the facts for her when I called her from Chicago. But as the plane took off, something happened. I began to hear Elicia's voice replay in my mind. My first instinct was to ignore it and stay focused on the task at hand; however, as her voice grew louder, I became sensitive to the hurt and pain packed into every word. As her words began to take root, nervousness began to fill the pit of my stomach. My heart started beating as fast as our rhythm of life. Then the unthinkable happened. Tears began to pour out of my eyes.

I had arrived at the doorway of brokenness.

My first step into brokenness was only the beginning of a six-year process God used to free me from the performance trap. During this time, God extended mercy to me in the form of a sabbatical from the pastorate. He began to provide rehab to my weary soul, showing me my lack of balance and how it tainted my assessment of His character. This slanted view of God was a prideful key inserted into my ignition of selfish ambition, fueling my actions to jump on the autobahn of a performance-driven life.

My heart was filled to the brim with suppressed hurt and pain rooted in my childhood. I was in dire need of shepherding. Although men in my church could have helped me, I was scared that if I let them in to my internal tensions they'd see me as a perpetual failure and fire me from my *job* of pastoring—though this thought was contrary to all of their character and their love for me. But as soon as I moved to Atlanta, I felt the overwhelming need to open my heart and expose my battle with the performance trap before men who loved Christ *and* were not members of the congregation I was the pastor of. And God, who knows all things, provided a way for me to receive it through transparent friendships with dear brothers in the faith. Just as how my older brother, Raymond, came alongside me when my dad abandoned me, my brothers in Christ living in Atlanta ran to my aid when I needed them most.

In this book I'm laying my heart on the line for two reasons. First: You're worth it. I bare the scars of all the mistakes I've made so that you can observe them, learn from them, and not make them. I value you as my brother or sister in Christ and entrust you with the content of my heart.

My second reason for laying it all out on the line? I want you to share in the freedom of being captured by God's grace as I have been. There's nothing more heartbreaking for me than to see saints living in the performance trap, not knowing there's a way out through the words of Christ. If you're there now, stay with me. This book will point you toward the truth that Christ wants to lead you out of this personal prison you were not sentenced to live in. The road to freedom is paved with Scripture and illuminated by God the Holy Spirit who desires to navigate you into the loving arms of Father God.

This message of freedom in grace is for all Christians, but I pray that my words are particularly timely to my fellow church planters and pastors and their families. For us, living in the performance trap can be the difference between life and death. Seventy-one percent of pastors reported to the Schaeffer Institute that they are burnt out and wrestle with depression daily, fifteen hundred of us leave the ministry each month because of moral failure or burnout, and 70 percent of pastors say they do not have at least one close friend.[2] And pastoral suicide is on the rise.[3]

Shortly after moving to Atlanta, I was stopped in my tracks one morning by a news report about a well-known and loved Atlanta pastor's recent suicide. My wife and I were glued to the television as his family shared about how they hadn't seen how much internal turmoil he was dealing with. When the reporter talked about the increasing frequency of pastoral suicide and symptoms to watch for, I was floored by how many symptoms were present in my own life!

Elicia asked me if I wrestled with what was being reported. I told her about a sermon John Piper preached about the life and ministry of David Brainerd and how Brainerd on at least twenty-two occasions asked God to take him home because of his battles with physical ailments and depressions.[4] When I told her I had prayed similar prayers, her eyes began to well up with tears. We prayed together, and she pleaded with me to share my heart with other brothers who were capable of shepherding me through this struggle. The content of this book is the result of the healing process.

By the Holy Spirit's empowering (Romans 8:9-13), you can walk in the freedom Christ has provided you with from sin and the encumbrances that weigh you down (Hebrews 12:1-2). I'm convinced that once you begin to realize that God's unfailing love is being poured out on you nonstop, you will naturally be compelled to proclaim the truth of the gospel to both saints and sinners. The fruit of your labor, when coupled with the supernatural work of God the Holy Spirit, will be made known through the disciples you raise up to enjoy the trap of God's grace. Freedom in Christ from the performance trap comes with a responsibility: to invite others into a relationship with Him and walk into maturity together with those whom He saves.

It's time to leave our striving for perfection behind. Let's walk in a balanced relationship with Christ according to His Word, all the while enjoying the life everlasting He's given to us upon regeneration.

PART 1

THE PERFORMANCE TRAP

TRAJECTORY

RELATIONSHIPS

AFFIRMATION

PEERS

Every believer willfully resides inside one of two traps: the performance trap or the trap of God's grace. In the performance trap, we run ourselves ragged trying to find *success*, all in the name of earning God's love. We maintain a lifestyle that's always on the go, and when we fail, we start seeing our holy God as a callous taskmaster who views us no longer as His *beloved* children but as disposable slaves.

And in the midst of the performance trap, we can easily fall into *self-induced legalism*. Self-induced legalists think they can earn a right standing with God by living a life of complete moral perfection. They externally bathe others in grace (unearned favor) while internally holding themselves to an impossible expectation: meeting the demands of their own subjective interpretation of God's righteous laws.

As a self-induced legalist, I used the alarm clock on my cell phone as a whip to "beat my body into submission." Every night before going to bed, no matter how early or late, I would set my alarm to wake me at 5:30 a.m. sharp. Even if I was shepherding in a crisis situation until 3:00 a.m., the law of 5:30 a.m. knew no mercy.

But when my alarm would go off at 5:30 a.m., I (normally exhausted from the day before) would walk over to my phone, turn off the alarm, and convince myself I'd sleep for only a few more minutes. When I woke up an hour or two later, I'd jump out of bed feeling as if I spent the last hour living in sin because I overslept! Most of my days started with me begging God to forgive me for being selfish, for choosing to sleep rather than pray and have a private devotional time. Needless to say, the remainder of my day was exhausting, as I would try to "work" myself back into a right relationship with God. Seriously, I felt like I wasn't back in good standing with God until I forced myself to fast from eating lunch.

I woke early most mornings to pray (most of the time interceding for other pastors and Christians), study Scripture, and meditate on the text I was working through. Yet despite this, I could not figure out how to *rest* in Christ's finished work on my behalf. My struggle with self-induced legalism caused me to believe that God was only pleased with me when I practiced my spiritual disciplines.

I would often look out the window of my legalistic cell and admire the freedom in Christ others had. I would congratulate the brothers and sisters in our local community and offer praises to God for their freedom—only to turn around and become enslaved by the thought, *I'm glad they are free, but I'll never be able to receive freedom like that.* Deep down I wanted out of this prison, but I never took time to realize that the door to my cell was unlocked and off the hinge! The gospel is the cure for self-induced legalism, and when I failed to remind myself daily of the gospel, I remained trapped in the performance-driven life.

You see, it's one thing to be used by God to communicate truth and see others benefit from it. It's another thing altogether to be the recipient of that same truth by applying it to your own life.

NAMING THE WALLS

When we're inside the performance trap, we can't see its framework, so we remain ignorant of our enslaved condition. But as God led me into grace, I began to see how the trap was shaped.

The performance trap has four walls. Together, these walls spell the word *trap*:

T: The first wall is our *trajectory* in life. This wall represents the direction our life is headed in as we pursue God's will.

R: The second wall deals with our *relationships*. It's constructed by the scars we've amassed from the emotional pain endured through all of our past failed relationships, from childhood to adulthood.

A: The third wall identifies our lack in receiving *affirmation*. Brick by brick we've built this wall out of all the insults that have been hurled at us over the years, and for the mortar we use the bitterness we feel from the lack of affirmation we've received from those we look up to.

P: The final wall is our internal competition with our *peers*. When we don't see the fruits that we desire in our ministries or our lives and yet see fruit in the lives of our friends and family members, we naturally tend to build a wall of hostility between them and us by comparing ourselves to them.

I have found that when my focus is on my trajectory, my relationships, my lack of affirmation, and the success of my peers, mental anguish hovers over me like my own personal rain cloud. It is during these times that I begin to doubt God's call in my life, my effectiveness for His glory, and even my call as a minister of the gospel. It's also during these times that I feel disconnected from both God and His Word, and the Scriptures become black-and-white words on pages that everyone else receives nourishment from except for me.

If you feel this way, there is hope. My conviction is this: If I can communicate the truth of God by coupling it with my own life's transparency, I believe God the Holy Spirit can do the transforming work in your heart that He alone is equipped to do. He can illuminate your heart to see not only the performance trap you're living in but also the exit sign you're being guided to.

Chapter 1

TRAJECTORY

PLANS CHANGE

Before Elicia and I were married, a trend in our dating relationship troubled me. Whenever we settled on plans to do anything, from seeing a movie to deciding whose family's house we would go to first on holidays, it was guaranteed 100 percent of the time that the plan would change.

The issue I had was not with the change itself but with a slight inconsistency that I began to notice. If I initiated the change, Elicia would express frustration, but if she was the one to change plans, my own frustrations went unheeded.

It's understandable for circumstances to change, because life is always in transition. In our day and age, most of us not only expect change but also try to plan for it, as oxymoronic as that sounds. Technology keeps us on our toes as we plug in an address on our phone's GPS only to be rerouted because of accidents or other unforeseeable incidents that happen along the way. Baseball games are rained out, and flights are delayed.

It's impossible to have everything in life go according to every plan we set. We all know there is a high probability that the plan we have in our minds won't come to pass exactly the way we always imagine. But we tend to hold on to the romantic, picture-perfect view of how we wanted our day to go. This tendency comes out in our attitude and how we treat others while we're dealing with disappointment.

Think about it: If this is how we treat our daily plans, how much more invested are we in our life's trajectory and our most dearly cherished dreams? When we face transitions that challenge our life's trajectory, we often cope by creating a romantic view of our trajectory and refusing to let it go. When we strongly desire to make our dreams reality, our flesh and all of its aspects (mind, will, and emotions) romanticize the steps needed to do so. Often this romanticized ideal has no connection to the reality of our current situation. Our goals have tangible and measurable signposts, but in our fantasies, all the stars align out of reach because we live on the ground and not in the clouds.

Please understand, I'm not saying we need to abandon our dreams. But when doors close and refuse to open, we must begin to assess whether the direction we want to go is in harmony with God's plan for our life. Our chief desire should be to glorify God by advancing the gospel message as we live in community with other saints and make disciples. This truth is a filter to safeguard our hearts as we consider our trajectory.

In my life, a respirator of willful ignorance kept my fantasies alive when I encountered challenges that hindered what I thought was my life's trajectory. Day after day, as the Lord would close doors and answer my prayers in ways I didn't want to hear, I kept refusing to pull the plug on my fantasies. I kept using isolated Scriptures as a tool of manipulation, thinking I could force God to give me what I was asking for. I quoted Psalm 37:4 and Proverbs 3:5-6 in my prayers, trying to hold God hostage until my fantasies became reality. I was convinced that my life *had* to go the way I imagined.

In conversations with other believers, I've noticed that my practice of fueling fantasy with Scripture is a common thread woven into the fabric of human hearts. We use an abundance of isolated Scriptures, presumptuous declarations, and decrees to distract ourselves from stewarding where we are in our walk with Christ. We search with a conspiracy theorist's passion for signs of *confirmation*—to the point where we'll find them even when they don't exist. We listen to the words people tell us and force-feed them into our fantasy in order to keep it alive. If we're not careful, when we merge these fantasies with the sense of God's calling on our lives, we can begin trying to convince ourselves and others that we are stepping out in faith because we know God's trajectory for our lives. When reality hits and the fantasy that, deep down inside, we knew was false finally ends, confusion begins to set in. We lose hope regarding our life's trajectory. Some who have landed here have walked away from their profession of faith in God, while others, like myself, will admit that this reality check was a needed wake-up call for their heart to be realigned with God's.

THE PRESSURE OF TRAJECTORY

When I speak about this wall in the performance trap called *trajectory*, I'm identifying the progress we make while traveling on life's path toward becoming what we're *supposed to be*. I'm fully convinced every believer shares the same God-given job description: the great commission (Matthew 28:19-20). We are all missionaries called by God to make Him famous in our world—and our mission field is every piece of ground that we walk on throughout the day. Where we live, work, and shop *is* our mission field.

Yet although we as the body of Christ bear this corporate calling, God has also provided each of us with the ability to be good at something in order to make an impact on the mission field He's placed us in. These individual gifts allow us to proclaim His excellence to those who appreciate our work. The question we all must ask is, "God, how do You want to use me for Your glory?" The answer to that question and how God leads us to do what He's called us to is what I call our life's *trajectory*. Please understand, not every Christian is called to lead or pastor a local church (1 Timothy 3:1-7; Titus 1:6-16) or be in professional ministry. We are all called to be excellent in our careers while impacting the area we live in through evangelistic and discipleship efforts that lead back to our local churches.

Our trajectory is not something sinful in itself, because most often it's what God has called us to do *while* we're living on a mission, making disciples of all ethnicities (the great commission). The danger we often face is when we lose balance, taking our eyes off Christ and instead fixing our gaze on the ideal destination we want to arrive at with or without Him. It is dangerous to assume God exists for our benefit instead of living a life for the sole purpose of glorifying Him (Isaiah 48:11; 1 Corinthians 6:20; 10:31; 1 Peter 4:11).

For some of us the destination is earning a degree from college, landing that dream job, writing a book, securing a record deal, starting a family, owning a home, planting a church, being in full-time ministry, or enjoying retirement. None of these destinations are in themselves sinful, but when we lack the correct perspective on our trajectory, our destination turns into a place of idolatry. We've allowed our hearts to stray from the course of life God desires to lead us on. We must regularly ask ourselves this gut-punching question: *Do I still want to arrive at my ideal destination if Jesus or His body, the church, isn't there?*

Surrounding the trajectory of our lives are three pressures that can distract us, causing us to take our eyes off Christ, remove our trust from God, and place it instead in our own abilities, gifts, and talents. These three pressures are the *tension*, *turmoil*, and *timing* of our trajectory.

Tension

We are constantly fighting the tension between what we desire to become, what others want us to become, and who Christ has called us to be. Sometimes we sense God leading us toward a specific destination, but we feel like the road to get there is taking too long. We find comfort in seeing the finish line from the starting line—but God doesn't always supply us with such a breathtaking view. In those times, we doubt Him, His Word, and even the calling He's placed on our lives.

To make matters more complex, family and friends often feel they have insight as to what our trajectory is. Conversations with them are filled with the dreams they have for us, and sometimes it seems as if they're trying to live vicariously through us. Phrases such as "if I were your age again," "I didn't have the opportunities you have," and "if I could do it all over, I would . . ." become cues for us to mentally check out of the conversation. These people mean well, but their comments and suggestions may block the clear picture of the future we once had in mind.

As I mentioned in the introduction, I spent thirteen years of my early life fully engaged in the sport of wrestling. By God's grace I had success early on, winning my first state championship at the age of seven. By my freshman year in high school, I had won five additional state championships, two regional runner-up silver medals, and the attention and interest of a few colleges. No one in my household had ever been to college, and my family didn't have the money to send me. So I was told at a young age that the only way I would be able to go to college was through wrestling. And growing up in a gang-infested neighborhood, I felt I had only three options for what to do with my life: join a gang, join the military, or go to college on a wrestling scholarship.

I couldn't join a gang because the Crips in my neighborhood who had dropped out of school wouldn't have my back while I attended a school that was dominated by Bloods, Latin Counts, and Spanish Disciples. My cousins and friends, with whom I spent most of my time, lived on the other side of town; joining their gang wouldn't make sense, because when I went back to my neighborhood I wouldn't have any backing. I didn't want to join the military because I didn't want to go through boot camp. So my only option was to be good enough at wrestling to earn a college scholarship.

Now, that doesn't sound like a bad plan . . . except for the fact that by the age of ten, I no longer loved wrestling. In fact, my hatred for it was so deep—the stress level to make weight, to win every single one of my matches, and to continue gaining national respect was so intense—that I started losing my hair. Simultaneously I found myself enduring severe stomach pains that sent me to the doctor repeatedly for MRIs, blood tests, and specialist consultations.

When my mom began to notice the missing patches of hair on my head, and the remnants in the bathroom trash can, she intervened. During the family talk that night, my mom and my dad asked me if I wanted to continue to wrestle. Now, for the outsider the easy answer was a simple no—but as you know from my story, I felt that if I said no I would lose my relationship with my dad. I also felt the pressure of knowing that the only way out of the poverty-stricken community I called home was wrestling—and don't neglect the fact that I only ten years old! So I said begrudgingly that I wanted to keep wrestling and that I would work to manage my stress better. I felt like I was on the verge of throwing my life away at a young age. I found myself competing in a grueling mental wrestling match. My opponent was the tension of my life's trajectory. The reward for winning this match wasn't a mere plaque; it was a successful life outside of the poor neighborhood I lived in and a chance to do something with my life other than become another statistic.

Sadly, I must confess that up until two years ago, I was still worried about my trajectory. The tension at that point in life dealt solely with my ministry. God allowed me to pastor an urban church, and I was offered more opportunities to speak at conferences and write books. The feedback and affirmation I received from people were based solely on my ministry endeavors. I became convinced that if I wanted to be embraced, I had to preach, rap, teach, and write as excellently as possible—and that if I didn't, I would lose my family, my friends, my church, and my relationship with God.

Conversations were one-way streets. People would walk away more confident in God while I stood there feeling like an ATM. People would press my buttons, get what they wanted by making a withdrawal, and walk away, leaving me alone until they needed to repeat the process. I felt like there was no escape from this attention because, after all, this was what God *called* me to do. My calling was beginning to feel more and more like a prison sentence instead of a privilege. I was being torn apart by the tension of what I thought people wanted from me and what I thought God wanted from me.

I'm the one who is to blame—not God or the precious people who sought me out for shepherding. My lack of balance in life and ministry kept me in a place where I was a glutton for punishment. Looking back, it's safe to say I was an ATM because I felt that I needed to flood my life conversations with *All Things Ministry* and nothing else.

As you know from the war going on in your soul, the struggle with the tension of life's trajectory is real. You know the depth of the dreams and calling God placed on your life for His glory, yet you can't see it through the nightmare of your current circumstances. In this tension we're prone to make God a genie in the Bible—we rub a few verses together that we've taken out of context, hoping they'll manipulate Him into making our future trajectory manifest itself immediately. I challenge you to avoid doing this, as it only furthers a distorted view of our God and His Word.

Instead, we must work through Scripture to identify God's pattern of using this tension to mature us spiritually. His desire for us is not instant gratification but rather growth in Christ as we walk out our faith with the saints in our church (Ephesians 4:11-16) and endure together whatever life throws our way (James 1:2-5). God has already determined our steps, and in our daily walk with Him we progressively *discover* what He's *determined*.

Embracing the tension of our trajectory helps us depend on God as we mature in Christ. And walking alongside brothers and sisters in our local body while we do this helps us work through the turmoil we face relating to our life's trajectory.

Turmoil

We can face turmoil regarding our life's trajectory because of the anxiety we feel about our stewardship of the spiritual gifts and talents God has blessed us with—and whom we're honestly looking to benefit while using them. First Corinthians 12:11 tells us, "One and the same Spirit is active in all these, distributing to each person as He wills." The word *these* in this verse points back to the gifts Paul listed in 12:8-10. Verses 4-7 identify God the Holy Spirit as the one who gives gifts to each and every believer as He determines. And as C. K. Barrett expresses, there are two benefits of God the Holy Spirit being solely responsible for believers' gifts: "so that none has occasion for boasting, or for a sense of inferiority."[1]

When it comes to using our Holy Spirit–given spiritual gifts, we must realize that our flesh can fall victim to pride. We distort the spiritual gifts the Holy Sprit has given us when we use them *solely* for personal edification or gain. In the entire context of 1 Corinthians 12–14, Paul communicates that the *primary* use of spiritual gifts should be in love, for the edification of the body of Christ. This includes 1 Corinthians 14:4, where Paul says, "Anyone who speaks in a tongue edifies themselves, but the one who prophesies edifies the church" (NIV).

Some scholars interpret "edifies themselves" as a positive action, while others see it as negative. Gordon Fee says that Paul was speaking in a positive manner regarding the "personal edifying of the believer that comes through private prayer and praise."[2] This interpretation doesn't fit the context Paul addresses, which is in a church service with other people present, not a person's personal time in prayer. Robert Wilkin says that Paul was speaking negatively about the gift of tongues being used for personal edification: "The person speaking in a tongue (uninterpreted) edifies [only] himself. He is not operating in love because love *does* not seek its own (1 Corinthians 13:5). The Corinthians must understand that the gifts are not given for personal enhancement or for building up their egos (cf. 1 Corinthians 12:7; 1 Peter 4:10-11)."[3]

Adding balance, Thomas Constable offers great insight as to *how* the person is edified:

> The person who spoke in tongues in church edified *only* "himself" or herself. He or she praised God and

prayed to God while speaking in a tongue. He or she also benefited from realizing that the Holy Spirit was enabling him or her to speak a language that he or she had not studied. This would have encouraged the tongues-speaker, but this speaker did not edify himself or herself in the sense of profiting *from the message* the Holy Spirit had given. He did not know what his own words meant unless he also had the gift of interpretation, but in this discussion Paul left that gift out of the picture almost entirely (cf. 1 Corinthians 14:5). Had he known what he was saying, he could have communicated this to those present in their language. . . . Paul's point was that edifying the church is more important than edifying oneself. He did not deny that speaking in tongues does on some level edify the tongues-speaker (cf. 1 Corinthians 14:14-15, 18-19).[4]

Constable believes, in essence, that the reality of a believer's edification is rooted in the fact that they are active in using the spiritual gift God blessed them with but that no one else would benefit from the use of the gift, and the church at large would not be edified.

I walk you through these different perspectives to show you that Paul's use of "edifies" suggests that the use of spiritual gifts is *primarily* for the edification of the Body and not *solely* for the building of a platform for the individual. When we begin to use the spiritual gifts given to us for our own personal advancement, we run the risk of becoming arrogant, thinking *we're* God's gift to the church. On the other hand, if we start comparing ourselves to our brothers and sisters in the Body who have been given different gifts, we may feel like second-class citizens in the Kingdom; the feeling of inferiority can lead us down the path of self-pity. Arrogance and inferiority create the turmoil we feel regarding our life's trajectory as it relates to our spiritual gifts. We're to counter these thoughts by remembering two truths: God the Holy Spirit distributes spiritual gifts as He desires, and the gifts we've been individually given should be used primarily for building up the saints in the local church.

In addition to all of this, God also provides each of us with various talents and natural abilities to do certain things with excellence, for His glory alone (1 Corinthians 10:31). Some of us have a giftedness to perform musically without ever having one lesson, while others have talents in the areas of academics, cooking, fine arts, or sports. Often with these talents comes a desire to improve our abilities, and we search for training and opportunities to hone the craft He's given us. There's nothing wrong with having been given a talent by God since every gift He gives is good (James 1:17). The challenge for us lies in stewarding our talent and, when we excel, giving all glory to the Lord instead of to ourselves.

Many saints who are dear to my heart have confirmed that God blessed me with a unique gifting in the area of communication. In elementary school, the music teacher pulled me aside one day and asked if I would accept the lead role in the school Christmas play. I didn't really understand what was going on, but I knew that I wanted to be on stage to entertain people (I was still an unbeliever at this point in my life). In the fourth grade I got my first taste of entertaining people and receiving praise for it, and I was hooked! Over the next several years I did anything and everything—from rapping to playing the trumpet—to get back out there on the stage. By high school I began to see that people paid attention to what I had to say . . . and to a pride-consumed, sinful heart, attention is the drug of choice.

The best example of this tendency happened my sophomore year of high school. My speech teacher told me I needed to stop blowing off my speech assignments and start getting credit for the gift of communication with which I was blessed. She said I was bound to flunk the semester but offered to cut me a deal: If I gave a demonstration speech, all would be forgiven for the *entire* semester, and I would get a passing grade. There was just one problem: I couldn't think of anything I could use as a prop for a demonstration. But when she asked if I had any books in my locker that had recently inspired me, I remembered the Bible in my backpack.

Now let me explain exactly why I had a Bible in my backpack. I had been raised in church since the age of five, and I was constantly told that if I were ashamed of Jesus, He would be ashamed of me on the last day. And I figured that one way to not be ashamed of Jesus was to carry a Bible with me at school. So I didn't really see the Bible as God's authoritative Word; rather, it was a good-luck charm that I kept in case someone asked me if I was ashamed of Jesus.

As I stood in front of the class with that Bible, I had no idea what I was going to say—but I knew I had to hit a home run to pass the class. Over the next ten minutes, I began to speak with conviction about the Bible being God's Word, regurgitating pieces of sermons I'd heard time and time again. When I was done, I said I believed the Bible was true and that's why I carried it with me.

At the end of my speech two extraordinary things happened. First, my entire class—made up of inner-city public school kids from the hood—sat utterly silent, staring at me. Silence in an inner-city classroom was a complete culture shock! Second, my teacher looked down at her grade book and began to move her shoulders almost uncontrollably. I initially thought she was laughing because my lifestyle didn't match anything I said. To my surprise, she took her glasses off before looking at me with tears streaming down her face! I couldn't believe it—this teacher, who had on a few occasions earlier in the semester kicked me out of class and threatened to call security on me, was crying.

She mumbled the word "beautiful" over and over before she was able to put together a full sentence: "Damon, that was absolutely beautiful! You are an extremely gifted communicator. This was one of the best sermons I have ever heard in my life!"

Now, you would assume I was moved with conviction by her affirmation—perhaps even moved to repent for my sins and get my life right with Christ. But that was not to be, at least on this day. Boastfully I responded, "So I'm getting an A, right?" Talk about arrogance personified. That was me, in the flesh, using my God-given talent for my own glory and not His.

After the Lord saved me, He began to work on my heart regarding proper stewardship of the gift of communication He blessed me with. But over the course of time, as He opened doors for me to preach and teach, I began to lose focus on stewarding the spiritual gift of teaching and the ability to communicate. I began to wrestle with wanting a greater platform, comparing myself to others and feeling inferior.

The more opportunities God provided me to preach or teach, the more angst I felt toward not being the "best" at using spiritual gifts for Christ's church. This angst was amplified because of my insecurity. As other saints and believers affirmed the spiritual gifts and talents God blessed me with, they would also seek to speak into my life by telling me what they thought God wanted to do through me for all of my days. Most often these words centered on our church growing in both membership and financial stability, me receiving greater opportunities through speaking in larger conferences, and me modeling what it looks like for American ethnic minorities indigenous to the urban core to obtain leadership status inside the world of evangelicalism.

Sometimes I was told I was going to be the next Francis Chan or John MacArthur but with an urban swag. Deep down I began to believe what others were saying, and once I allowed my mind to run away with their words, a disconnection from reality took place, and the affair with a fantasy ministry began. The turmoil I faced forced me to wrestle daily with insecurities that had previously been nonexistent. If a conference didn't invite me back the next year, I felt like a failure. If months went by without someone asking me to preach or teach somewhere, I thought God no longer wanted to use me because of some *secret* sin I couldn't identify. Turmoil fed pride's hunger in my heart. Daily I confessed any and every sin I could think of, even going back into my childhood. I was sure that once I found the hidden sin still staining my record before God, He'd open the doors of heaven and bless me with more opportunities to minister.

Living in the performance trap can cause our minds to run a mile a minute when we lie down at night. As we toss and turn, turmoil causes us to dwell on thoughts contrary to the gospel. We question God's love for us and assume He's forgotten us. If we give in to turmoil, we'll try to rush God's plan, attempting to open doors in our own strength because our omniscient Father seems off with His timing and needs our help.

Timing

In the performance trap, tension and turmoil combine to serve as the double-edged sword that lodges deep in the heart of our ambition. With every life movement we make, the sword drives deeper into our souls, causing restless pain. We can live in fear that making one wrong decision will ultimately cancel out the trajectory others sense for our lives. Fear can paralyze us to the point that we feel we can't make any substantial decisions in life unless we have the comfort of at least a dozen people affirming our decisions. When I was in the midst of this anxiety, I constantly asked God *when* what others saw would become a reality. When I felt like I wasn't following in the footsteps of both Chan and MacArthur, a sense of pain would consume me as if life had passed me by and God had written me off as damaged goods.

What got me through these times were fantasies about what seemed to be "around the next corner" in life. These fantasies served as my emotional painkiller.

But I began to grow immune to the regular dose of fantasy, as happens with any painkiller, and I needed something more. At the same time, I saw no sign of what people were saying my trajectory was. I felt like a failure. The season of harvesting and seeing an increase evaded me daily. During times of private prayer I asked God why people identified fruitfulness as part of His trajectory for my life while I felt sentenced to a ministry filled with laborious plowing, planting, and watering that rarely produced any fruit.

The pressure of the timing weighed me down emotionally. My daily opponent was the idea that I was another millennial who suffered from having big dreams and little success. Worry and doubt must have tracked me down on Twitter because they both followed me every minute of every day, *favoriting* and *retweeting* every one of my insecurities. If anything I've shared resonates with your heart as it does for me, then you know this pressure is real and that it cripples us to the point that we paralyze ourselves from being effective agents of God's grace.

You may feel paralyzed in your walk with Christ because you're making seemingly little progress toward what you sense God has called you to do. Anxiety, doubt, and frustration might have your heart flirting with thoughts of giving up, throwing in the towel, no longer being faithful to God or His body, the church. In those moments of spiritual warfare, I challenge you to follow the apostle Paul's instructions in Ephesians 6:17: "Take the helmet of salvation, and the sword of the Spirit, which is God's word." Paul challenges us to guard the most vulnerable part of our body: our mind.

How do we do this? By taking every one of our thoughts captive to Christ (2 Corinthians 10:5) and dwelling on things that edify us (Philippians 4:8). Whenever we think God has stopped loving us, has abandoned us, or is not pleased with us, we are to take those very thoughts and compare them to God's Word. If our thoughts are true, they will line up with Scripture. But if our thoughts are not supported in God's Word—and thoughts that make us feel paralyzed in our faith are not!—we must reject and renounce them. The key to victory in these moments is reading God's Word, memorizing it, and quoting it. The perfect model we have of this practice is Jesus in Matthew 4:1-11. When Satan tempted Him, He didn't physically beat Satan down, nor did He call on legions of angels to take care of Satan. Instead, He quoted Scripture. Scripture provides us with profound insight about how to respond to the tension, turmoil, and timing of our trajectories.

THE TRAJECTORY OF ABRAHAM

Abraham's story in Scripture speaks to those of us trying to navigate through life while dealing with the pressure of our life's trajectory. God asked Abraham to leave the country that he knew because He was going to bless him by making him a great nation (Genesis 12–15). God also promised Abraham that his family line would serve as a blessing to all the nations on earth—and indeed, his story points us to an eternal hope in God that was promised through the person and work of Jesus Christ. Abraham provides us with a model of what it looks like to trust God while enduring the pressures of tension, turmoil, and timing.

Abraham's Response to the Tension

In Genesis 12:2-3, God asked Abraham to go somewhere he had never been and to stay in a place that was uncomfortable. At this point, Abraham was seventy-five years old. It's not as if God came to Abraham with this message while he was young, when life would have been a little bit more flexible. Put yourself in Abraham's shoes. In that season of life, you wouldn't be dealing with SAT or ACT scores, varsity tryouts, or social media updates. Or contemplating whom you're going to marry or what career you should consider going into. Or focusing on signing the final documents to secure a home loan or working sixty-plus hours a week in order to climb the corporate ladder. And you wouldn't be settling into the new normal of retirement, ushered in by an empty nest and an RV purchase.

Rather, our text identifies Abraham within a time of life where permanency, not transition, is the goal. Certainly he must have felt the tension between what God was calling him to do and what everyone else in his culture expected of him. As uncomfortable as it was for Abraham to receive those instructions from God, he still chose to obey God's call, leaving his lifelong comfort zone.

Remember, the tension in our life involves our calling from God as well as what others want our life to look like. Our initial call from God was to the Cross, so that we might receive salvation through the work of Christ. We once spent our lives running from grace, and then all of a sudden we heard the gospel preached and were moved by God the Holy Spirit to put our trust in the work of Jesus and be born again (John 3:3-8).

Perhaps our family and friends had no issues with us *finding religion*, but over the course of time when they saw a genuine change in us, they may have begun to express doubts because seriously following God looks like giving up a life that chiefly pursues personal comfort and pleasure.

God's commands have been known to shake up the life trajectories of those who follow Him. The goal is to focus not on the trajectory we desire but on obeying God's command. In Abraham's case, he was commanded to move away from his entire family. Imagine the tension when he dropped this news on everyone at the dinner table! The Bible doesn't capture such a moment, but I assume the air was filled with more than awkward silence. Yet despite whatever resistance he got from family and even his wife, Abraham chose to push through the tension by obeying God.

Abraham's Response to the Turmoil

When we get to Genesis 15:2-3, we see that the question Abraham asked earlier—*what would You give me?*—has now transitioned into a declaration: *You haven't given me anything.* This transition is the unveiling of turmoil. We sense God leading our life in a specific direction, we have a desire to obey God by using our spiritual gifts, but we're not making any progress toward our trajectory being realized. Like Abraham, our *yes, Lord* turns into *when, Lord?* It's here where insecurities cause us to question our identity in Christ—to the point where we may begin to wonder if we're even saved!

Abraham probably struggled with something like this. There's a ten-year gap between Genesis 15:2-3 and Genesis 16:3. Abraham was now a vivacious eighty-five-year-old who had endured a decade of constant transition. Yet in the midst of this turmoil, Abraham continued to believe God and obey Him, even when there was still no child given to him and his wife as God had promised.

There are times in life when we see the promises of God as being delayed—but what we see as God's *procrastination* is actually His *preparation* of our hearts so we will be able to steward well what He blesses us with. In Abraham's case, God was preparing him the son who would end up being in the lineage of Jesus Christ. This type of realized promise would take a great deal of stewardship—not some haphazard fleeting excitement that fades when the newness wears off. It does us good to wait patiently for God during our season of preparation.

Abraham's Response to the Timing

In Genesis 21:5, Abraham finally receives his promised son, Isaac. By this time, Abraham is a hundred years old. Let's look at the timeline: Abraham received a promise at the age of seventy-five that was not realized until the age of one hundred. Let this sink in—what took you and me five minutes to read took Abraham twenty-five years to live! That's twenty-five years of failures and victories, lows and highs captured for you and me to learn from. Although Abraham did not perfectly obey God, God's grace saw him through a life filled with simple mistakes. And as I said earlier, I believe his story remains today to point us not to his success but rather to God's faithfulness to keep His promises—specifically through the incarnation of Jesus Christ, who was born in the line of Abraham. God's timing is perfect, and it is part of a plan we can't begin to fathom.

THE PRESCRIPTION FROM SCRIPTURE

Since Abraham's story points us to Christ, let's fast-forward out of the Old and into the New Testament to Romans 4:20-24, where we see how Abraham's response directly affects those of us who are in Christ:

> He did not waver in unbelief at God's promise but was strengthened in his faith and gave glory to God, because he was fully convinced that what He had promised He was also able to perform. Therefore, it was credited to him for righteousness. Now *it was credited to him* was not written for Abraham alone, but also for us. [Emphasis added]

The word *credited* was used frequently in the financial world of Paul's day, communicating the action someone performed when he put money into another person's bank account.[5] Paul used this word to unpack the reality that Abraham's belief was not in himself, because he was too old to father a child. Rather, his belief was in God. Abraham believed that God's promise in Genesis 12 was something he would receive simply because God said it. The Scripture tells us that before Abraham received what God promised him, he already believed God, who then credited Abraham with righteousness.

As you look at the passage, take notice of the phrase "it was credited to him was not written for Abraham alone, but also for us" (Romans 4:23-24). This truth parallels nicely with Romans 15:4, which says, "Whatever was written in the past was written for our instruction, so that we may have hope through endurance and through the encouragement from the Scriptures." The word Paul used for *endurance* means "the capacity to hold out or bear up in the face of difficulty."[6] God has provided us with encouragement during those seasons in life when we're questioning our trajectory because we feel like our fate keeps avoiding us. According to Paul, the narrative of saints in the Scriptures was documented to give us models of what endurance looks like in the face of the tension, turmoil, and timing of our trajectory. So when you're battling fear, doubt, and unbelief, get into the Scriptures and learn from the lives of other saints.

We must work to realize that, like Abraham, all of us were born spiritually in debt because of sin. We were not righteous; in fact, we were the opposite. We should be encouraged by Abraham's story—he serves as a model for what it looks like to believe in God and have our debt wiped away and replaced by a deposit of righteousness into our account.

You see, we were all born in a state of guilt before God because we inherited a sinful nature from Adam (Romans 5:12) and were seasoned sinners because it enslaved us (John 8:34). While in this state of being, we did not have the innate ability to change ourselves. We needed to believe what

God has said regarding how we can be "declared righteous." The only way for us to be declared righteous is by believing that Jesus Christ is the only qualified Savior to save sinners out of their state of sinfulness (John 14:6). We're declaring spiritual bankruptcy.

What happens next is truly amazing. God meets us where we are, hears our cry of spiritual bankruptcy, forgives us for our sins, and then credits to our account an unlimited amount of righteousness! The righteousness we are given comes directly from Jesus Christ, who is Abraham's promise realized. So what we must understand is that when we embraced Christ as Savior, God not only forgave us for our sins but also clothed us in the righteousness of Christ. When He sees us, He sees the perfect life of Christ that covers us (Romans 13:14; Galatians 3:27).

So what does all of this have to do with trajectory? Our life's trajectory should not be focused on what others want us to become or even on what we want to become, especially if our desires are not in harmony with making disciples. We should no longer fuel our fantasies with romantic future plans that are unlikely to become reality. Rather, in our life's trajectory we should focus on gaining a greater understanding of who we are in Christ Jesus. As we understand who we are in Christ, we will become content in the journey of life on which God walks with us while we're living in community with other saints in our local body.

By understanding our identity in Christ, we will apply the endurance we've been given by God to persevere through the season of preparation in which God has positioned us. With our identity in Christ at the forefront of our mind, we'll rejoice during our seemingly endless seasons of plowing, planting, and watering. In Christ alone will we be able to enjoy a freedom from the pressure of our trajectory and a renewed trust in God.

Chapter 2

RELATIONSHIPS

WE'RE RELATIONAL BEINGS

One truth I love about our God is that for all of eternity, He has been in community. He has always simultaneously existed as Father, Son, and Holy Spirit. Although the Bible never specifically uses the word *Trinity*, we can rest assured that throughout all of Scripture, the doctrine of the triune nature of the Godhead is expressed regularly (Genesis 1:26; 3:22; Isaiah 6:8; Matthew 3:16-17; 28:19-20; 2 Corinthians 13:13; Ephesians 1:3-14). Simply put, God exists in community and created humans to have fellowship with Him inside this perfect community. A community cannot exist without relationships—and so God is serious about relationships.

The first time in all of Scripture where God says something is not good is in Genesis 2:18: "It is not good for the man to be alone." Adam was living in an environment without a relationship with another created being who shared the image of God. God purposefully withheld certain of His characteristics from all other forms of creation in order to exclusively share them with human beings, His crowning act of creation. Because of this, I can honestly say that when we live in isolation, we are living contrary not only to the plan of God for our life but to God's very nature. *Relationships are important.*

It's only natural, then, that the second wall in the performance trap is built out of our relationships. In the performance trap, we feel a heaviness to please those we love and want acceptance from. Because of the Fall, sin is present in every relationship, which means there's a high risk of abuse, hurt, or abandonment. We naturally tend to leverage our scars as reasons to protect ourselves from being hurt again.

Three common relationship scars can make up this wall of the performance trap. Daily we're working through relationship issues rooted in wounds that have been dealt to us by our *parents*, *peers*, and *potential partners* in relationships that range from dating to business to ministry. Let's take time to process each of these scars.

Parents

Facing the scars in our hearts caused by our parents is tough. It arouses painful memories we've worked hard over the years to bury under the ashes of burnt bridges. I have yet to meet anyone who has not received scars from the mistakes made by those who were responsible for their upbringing. Those emotional injuries happened for the same reason that others incur injuries from their own actions and words: We're all sinful humans who are prone to make mistakes.

We all have unique childhood narratives, yet we share hurts common to all humans, such as broken promises, neglect, various forms of abuse, and even abandonment. These hurts then naturally fuel our desire to build walls of self-preservation that we hope will prevent us from being injured again. The danger in building such walls is that we naturally thrust the consequences of our hurts onto God. If we had a poor relationship (if any) with our earthly father, we tend to shudder at the thought of God being our spiritual and heavenly Father. For many of us, the thought of God as "Father" doesn't make any sense.

Whether we experienced the reality of blended families, single-parent homes, the foster-care system, or two-parent homes—or abuse in any of those—we often struggle with the feeling that God will treat us how we were treated growing up. When we hear others refer to God as Father as a term of endearment, we can wonder why someone would want God to share a title that we associate with deep pain.

As I mentioned at the beginning of this book, my relationship with my dad while I was growing up and coming of age was not the best. I would be lying if I said the residue of that pain didn't resurface as I reflected on that long-ago wrestling tournament. For the majority of my walk with Christ, I've naturally carried the baggage from my relationship with my dad into my relationship with God. Because of this, for years I prevented myself from seeing God as a loving Father because I didn't see my earthly dad in that light. Just as I feared that my dad would abandon me, I assumed that God the Father would abandon me if I disappointed Him.

Now that I'm the father of three precious children, I bear the weight of how my imperfections taint their view of God. My heart aches every time I hear them confess that they feel like God has kicked them out of His family because they got in trouble for fighting with one another or for lying about cleaning their room. I have lost count of how many times my daughters have shared with me their fear of God abandoning them because they are not perfect.

One morning, my oldest daughter, Izabelle, woke up with an attitude because she couldn't have her favorite cereal for breakfast. Elicia and I addressed her ungratefulness and told her there were many kids who woke up in Atlanta without food in their entire house. Then before lunch she instigated a fight with her younger sister, Lola, that ended with both girls getting a spanking. After both girls were disciplined, Elicia and I talked to them about how and why they are to respect each other and how they have no right to talk to each other with hurtful words. And as if matters couldn't get any worse, right before our family evening prayers, Izabelle grew irritated again with Lola regarding a small matter and chose to make a big deal out of it.

At this point, Elicia and I were frustrated with both girls and sent them to bed with one assignment: to ask God for forgiveness and for help with not repeating their actions the next day. After the girls walked out, Elicia and I looked at each other and started talking about how to deal with the girls when we had days like this. But then our conversation came to a screeching halt as a piece of folded notebook paper slid under our bedroom door. I walked over, picked it up, and brought it to our bed so Elicia and I could read it together.

It was a letter from both girls, explaining how they were not worthy to be part of our family. They had talked it over and felt it would be best if we dropped them off at an orphanage and picked up two other daughters who would better appreciate being part of our family. They closed the letter by saying they were packing their things and would be ready to be replaced in the morning.

Naturally after reading this, both of our hearts sank. We knew it had been a rough day, but never would we want to give our girls away or replace them. We were stunned they would come to this conclusion. Immediately we went to the girls' bedroom, turned on the light, and reaffirmed our unconditional love for them, telling them how God sent them into our lives as blessings and gifts.

You would've thought this affirmation would have ended all the *give us away* talk, but they've expressed this same concern half a dozen times since this occurrence. Over time Elicia and I noticed that their sincerity had turned into a ploy to distract us from ever disciplining them. They were reassured of our love but, out of the sinfulness of their hearts, were trying to find a way to evade punishment by over-punishing themselves.

We believers do the same thing! Self-induced legalism masks itself as condemnation when conviction over sin becomes real. Believers must learn the difference between conviction and condemnation. Conviction will draw us back to God as we confess our sins, repent, and receive His forgiveness through the shed blood of Christ (Ephesians 1:7; Colossians 1:13-14). Condemnation causes us to run from God so we can attempt to live right for a while before attempting to approach Him. The problem with condemnation is that it keeps us from ever feeling like we're living holy lives, and so we choose to stay distant from God. Over time, self-induced legalism encourages us to beat God to the punch regarding discipline. We feel that if we abuse and punish ourselves, God will be manipulated into forgiving us before we ask, not dealing with our sin because we already dealt with it.

Once the Lord saved me, I thought I had to live a perfect life to keep Him happy with me. When I say perfect, I literally mean *perfect*. I was convinced that if I committed any sin, even in ignorance—and I mean even the smallest infraction against God's commands—God would abandon me. My walk with Christ was not one filled with joy, peace, and happiness. Rather, it was filled with an understanding that if I didn't perform perfectly for him, God the Father would, like my dad, abandon me because my less-than-perfect performance would render me unworthy to be His son.

Peers

As if the scars we received from our parents/guardians weren't enough, the unique challenges of our relationships with peers add another level of complexity to this wall in the performance trap.

In my time conversing with saints in cities across our nation,

I've noticed a trend: the coexistence of *circles* and *cliques* in churches. There is a thin line between a circle and a clique. They both include people who share common interests and are often seen fellowshipping both inside and outside the church. The distinction? One is *inclusive* and the other *exclusive*.

Allow me to provide an example. A circle of friends in a church could be a group of homeschooling families who meet regularly for encouragement, curriculum ideas, and the opportunity to discuss current state legislation as it relates to homeschooling. If the homeschooling circle both invites and allows non-homeschooling families to fellowship with them, they remain a circle, but if they criticize and ostracize those families who do not homeschool, they've become a clique.

In American church culture, something as innocent as a Sunday school class can start out as a circle—but over the course of time it can become a clique if the hearts of the circle do not remain welcoming to others. Hypocrisy is often born within this reality as people begin to wear different masks around different circles or cliques, seeking acceptance from their peers. I have personally witnessed seasoned saints well into their sixties, as well as preteens, attempt to navigate this tension in order to please their peers inside the church.

The most grievous outcome I've witnessed is when people

have desired to be embraced by a circle or clique in a church, worn the mask of *Christian* for an extended amount of time, eventually got tired of the hypocrisy of their life, and abruptly removed themselves from fellowship with the ones they tried so hard to be accepted by. I've seen this a lot in youth groups. Teenagers make a profession of faith in Jesus and attempt to walk away from their former life by diving headfirst into the pool of peers known as the *in-crowd* of the youth group. As students stick around, they begin to learn the Christian language of the youth group attendees, notice who is popular, and often work hard to get plugged into the social pipeline that leads to direct access to the pastor, leader, or director. These students do this because, like all human beings, they desire meaningful relationships.

The youth group I was blessed to be a part of while growing up was unique in many ways. Our average Wednesday night attendance ranged between 600 and 800 students, made up mostly of inner-city teens from across the entire Kansas City metropolitan area. Our auditorium had it all—flashing lights, state-of-the-art sound systems, fog machines, and big screens for projecting lyrics to worship-song videos and whatever was happening on stage. We had dance and drama teams; about a dozen different rap groups; a traveling youth choir; and our own logo, T-shirts, chant, and hand signs. Whenever we traveled anywhere as a group, people noticed us. Our goal was to set the rhythm for the entire atmosphere.

If an average teen with artistic talents visited our service on any given Wednesday night, our atmosphere drew his or her heart in immediately. But not just anyone could get on the stage. To be on stage, you had to make a profession of faith and then follow up with a commitment to go through the new-members class. Upon graduation you could then choose which ministry you wanted to join.

Out of the regular 600 to 800 weekly attendees, about 100 were a part of what regular attendees called the *inner circle*, and within this *inner circle* were smaller circles and cliques. The rappers would hang out with the rappers and the dancers with the dancers, and if you went to the same school, that was another bullet point on your résumé of acceptance. When we'd gather together for prayer or go on trips, these subcultural walls of separation appeared to have fallen down. However, when we had down time, the cliques would surface, meet up, and hang tight for the day. Almost always, drama would follow us wherever we went because of a slip of the tongue here, a cutting of the eyes there. Or the gossip about a person in another clique would grow from a small fire into a raging inferno. And the complexities of the dating relationships in the group always guaranteed some form of drama.

Our youth leaders and pastors would mediate whenever conflicts or issues of PDA (public displays of affection) surfaced.

We were youth and we had issues. What I realize now that I didn't realize then was the amount of pressure we all felt. People from every clique felt they had to perform—do the right things—in order to maintain a good standing with the *inner circle*. I wasn't privy to this reality until people began to open up to me when we were in our twenties about the pressures they felt during our teen years together. The pressures could range anywhere from raising hands during slow worship songs in order to be perceived as being more spiritual, to talking to or dating a person who was popular in order to be accepted by others who were more popular. Much to my sadness, people shared that I had contributed greatly to the pressure because of my dishonest, immature, or sarcastic remarks.

Of all the conversations I've had pertaining to *life after youth group*, one with a dear friend of mine stands out. He was invited to our youth group during the week we called our school tour. For one week each fall, our youth pastor would bring in a national act from the Christian music scene and a motivational speaker to minister in anywhere from ten to fifteen public schools around the Kansas City metropolitan area. This young man attended one of the schools we visited and accepted an invitation to come to our evening rally later that same night.

He was raised in the church and admitted that when he first walked into our service he loved what he saw. That evening he came forward, made a profession of faith in Christ, and asked how he could join our church and be part of the youth ministry. He was gifted with many talents, so he fit right in. Shortly after he joined the drama team that I was a part of, we began to hang out more and realized that we both liked the same type of hip-hop music. On a regular basis we would exchange rhymes that we wrote. I introduced him to the members of the rap group that I was a part of, and he said he was looking to start a rap group as well.

Over the next six years, he and I would share the gospel together on stages all across the country, hang out in each other's homes, and even serve alongside each other in youth ministry as leaders while we were in our early twenties. He was right by my side when I accepted my first youth pastor position, serving as my assistant. When I felt the Lord was moving me to a different church, I met with him and asked if he would take over the youth group we were currently serving together. He and his wife prayed about it and agreed. I felt led to accept the new position, so I transitioned out. We stayed in contact regularly for the next year and half—and then all of a sudden the phone calls and text messages came to a stop.

I didn't think much of it because I was now married with a child, and he and his wife were about to have their first child—I figured we were growing into adulthood and needed to focus on our families. Every now and then I would check up on them and ask how he was doing; he would respond by telling me that he was *hanging in there* and *trying to make a dollar out of fifteen cents*. He never really unpacked some of the struggles that he was going through, but soon I found out what was going on when I received a phone call from one of our mutual friends.

This phone call caused me to sit down and reflect on my friend's life trajectory. Our mutual acquaintance told me that my friend and the rap group he was a part of had made a complete 180-degree turn away from proclaiming the gospel; they were now talking about the typical street-life episodes the average rapper in our city would boast in. At first I didn't believe it. I thought that the call was a prank. But then I looked at his website, and I was hit with the reality of what I had been told. My heart began to ache with an unceasing grief.

Immediately I reached out to him through phone calls and text messages but didn't receive any response. I even commented on his website and sent him an e-mail to see if we could meet up and talk. Still he gave me no response. Not knowing what to do next, I decided to put the questions that were on my heart into a song. That night I wrote, recorded, and released online a song to him and another brother in his group, asking them my questions and challenging them about the direction of their lives.

Many of the young adults I was around who were also together with us in our youth group expressed appreciation for the content of the song's lyrics. They valued the relationship I had with our mutual friend and prayed God would move on his heart to carve out time for me. A few people who were still in communication with him challenged him to sit down and talk to me. When he finally reached out, he told me life was on hold because his newborn son was having a lot of complications, and he and his wife were literally living at the hospital. I asked if we could just link up for lunch so that I could express my love for him and his family, ask him what happened, and pray with him about his son's health. Eagerly he responded like he always used to and said he would love to see me.

We met that same afternoon at a Wendy's in Midtown near the hospital where his son was. We sat there for hours, reminiscing about our past adventures, our present struggles, and our future desires to be in ministry. In this conversation he made his heart completely vulnerable to me, unpacking all of the issues that he had endured as the youth pastor of the church I left him in charge of. He expressed in great detail the grief in his heart and the unique challenges of urban youth ministry that he felt he wasn't prepared for. He went on to share that his reason for changing paths was the result of a lack of financial stability in urban youth ministry. After the bills kept piling up, he felt the need to secure resources that would allow his family to have food on the table and a roof over their head.

I told him I understood that struggle but was puzzled by his drastic change in lifestyle. It was at this point that he made plain the peer pressure he felt from day one in our youth group. He had felt a heaviness to perform like a Christian whenever he was around our peers, and then when he left the youth group environment, he felt an equally stressful burden to maintain his street credibility. He said he appreciated the time in our youth group and often bragged to the youth he was pastoring about the great things we did in ministry, but he had buckled under the pressure that the streets had put on him in order to feed his family. He no longer wanted to be fake. He was angry at the church because he felt that they only loved the performer they saw on Sundays and Wednesdays—and that when they began to see the real him, the love disappeared. He felt abandoned.

He thanked me for taking time out of my day and away from my family to meet with him and told me that he knew that I loved him. He said he missed the days of youth group, but they were in the past and now he had to look toward the future. Then he dropped a bomb on me that was so damaging to my heart that I'm still trying to heal from it to this day. He looked into my eyes and told me, "Damon, listen. I'm only out here doing my music so that I can make one commercial hit.

After I make that hit, I'm gonna stack my money and go back into ministry with you full-time, and we're gonna change our city!"

What hurt most about what he shared was not the fact that he was no longer in *paid* full-time ministry, or that he felt hurt and abandoned by people who professed Christ. No, what cut my heart deeply was that he put the mission we were once sold out to on hold because the money wasn't there. Every believer is a full-time missionary. We all have the same job description—the great commission—and have been *on the clock* from the moment of our conversion. We shouldn't put our involvement in evangelism, disciple-making, and personal holiness on hiatus because of a lack of finances.

After our time together, we went our separate ways, only talking three times over the next nine years. Whenever he called out to me, I responded by running to him. Each of those three times we talked, he assured me that his commercial hit was coming and that he and I would be back in ministry together soon.

I weep as I type this, because two years ago he died.

I got the text while I was on the road, traveling to minister in Philadelphia. As soon as my plane landed, my phone started buzzing so much that people were looking at me as if I were ignoring a persistent caller.

When I read the text message that informed me he had just passed away, my fast-paced life came to a halt. I had no words. The pain that welled up in my soul was too deep. I sat in the Philadelphia airport in a daze, not knowing how to call my wife and tell her the grievous news. I didn't even know how to pray and couldn't concentrate on preparing to preach later that evening. When I finally made it to my hotel, I broke down and cried out to God, asking Him why this had happened. My heart poured out prayers for my friend's wife and his two precious sons. Looking back, I praise God for Romans 8:26, which says, "In the same way the Spirit also joins to help in our weakness, because we do not know what to pray for as we should, but the Spirit Himself intercedes for us with unspoken groanings." As I was stumbling through my grief-filled prayer, God the Holy Spirit was making perfect intercession to the Father on my behalf. His ministry in the moment carried me through my grief.

At the time of his death, my friend still hadn't released a commercial hit. He never rejoined me in ministry. His words of confession still ring loud in the space of my memory. Sometimes it's like I can still hear him express how tired he was of performing for his peers at church, which caused him to walk away—only to live under the conviction that he could come back on his own terms.

I pray that we as the body of Christ create space for saints to be transparent among their peers in our local churches. A transparency where we welcome the confession of sin, where we embrace and love the repentant saint while he or she is being restored into a place of spiritual maturity. And within this, we must allow space for our own confession of sin and fleshly struggles as well. It's important for us to understand that the pressure to perform for the acceptance of peers is not just a teenage issue; it's a human issue. God has created us to live in community, and as the body of Christ, we should model what healthy communal relationships look like. There's no better way to do this than by embracing people with all their flaws, loving them as they are, and walking with them while pursuing maturity in Christ together.

Potential Partners

The final piece of the relationship wall deals with those who are our potential partners in ministry or business or marriage. The pressure we often feel in these potential relationships deals with the question, "Will they like me—the real me?" I believe that every human being has the same desire: to be fully known and still fully loved. It's easy for us to put on our best front when we are going out on the first date or when we are meeting together in our first brainstorming session. When we begin to receive affirmation from that potential partner, we feel euphoric knowing that they like us. But this bliss ends quickly when we realize that in order to keep them liking us, we have to top our presentation/performance from today.

Think about Instagram for a moment. We'll take a series of pictures (mostly selfies) on our phones and select the best out of the dozens that don't meet our expectations. Once we select the photo we're most comfortable with, we realize it's still not perfect, so we decide to crop and edit it before posting it. In essence, we put on display our *best* (albeit doctored up to look good). We'll either then delete the dozens of photos that didn't make our feed or keep them hidden in our gallery. And the people who follow us are impressed by how picture perfect our life looks.

And sometimes, our lives can be like an Instagram feed. We go through great pains to doctor ourselves up emotionally, mentally, and physically before we step out the door. By doing this, we control what others can see—and what we want them to see is our best. All the while we keep the real us hidden safely in the gallery of our hearts. We protect our hearts in the same way we keep our phones protected by a password. We may reluctantly give our heart's password to those we trust, but if they hurt us, and our relationship breaks apart, we'll change the password and make the next person work twice as hard to earn access to the *real us.*

Since we've all endured the pain of broken relationships, we tend to carry our baggage and scars into the rebound relationship we're accustomed to running to for "healing." If we stick in this rebound relationship long enough, we begin to let our internal guard down and identify this person as our new *potential*. Sadly when this relationship self-destructs, our once-new potential is quickly added to the list of old flames or partners, and often in anger we burn the bridges that connect us to them. We move on from one potential to another until our hearts are hardened and we push away real love or partnership when it finally arrives on the scene.

Suspicion becomes our best friend. If we're honest, our hurt prevents us from trusting anyone, including ourselves. We're so fearful of being hurt that we'll only allow relationships to get to a certain point. As we refuse to cross the enigmatic "point of no return," we begin to officially withdraw from the relationship by injecting bad attitudes into delightful evenings. We respond with abrupt and direct answers to questions that our potential partner is sincerely asking, and we spend more and more time away from him or her.

We become so tired of all our failed relationships that we're not sure we have the endurance to enter into something with a hint of permanence. Our fear of commitment begins to drive our emotions, and we may pull out of a relationship simply because we assume it's going to end badly, just like all the others.

Our jaded past affects not only our interpersonal relationships but also our relationship with God. We begin to operate under the false assumption that we can walk in and out of a relationship with Him as we please. We flirt with the idea of having a relational breakthrough with God but refuse to press through our heart's breaking point. We hold Him at bay by never giving Him our past relational baggage.

THE PERFORMANCE OF JESUS

It's life's greatest quandary. We were created by God to have fellowship with Him, and since He placed eternity in our hearts (Ecclesiastes 3:11), we long to be connected to Him who is eternal. But since we're sinners, our innate affection for the eternal has been tainted, and we insanely pursue temporary pleasures, hoping they'll provide us eternal satisfaction. Since God is holy and we are sinful, we are separated from Him—and rather than running to Him, we naturally run away from Him in order to chase after the pleasures the world offers us (Romans 3:9-18).

The answer to this quandary is found in the person and work of Jesus Christ alone. He who has always been fully God willingly added to His full deity full humanity so He could pay our ransom, buying sinners out of slavery in order to bring us back into a right relationship with God.

I've been blessed to have walked with Christ for nineteen years now. Yet seventeen of those years were spent under the false assumption that I needed to perform perfectly in order to stay in a relationship with God. Notice I said *false assumption*—that phrasing is intentional, because the Bible tells us the truth from God's objective view, not man's subjective opinion. Scripture is clear that the only performance that matters when it comes to gaining God's affection is the performance of Jesus Christ. So as God the Father draws sinners to the cross of Jesus Christ (John 6:44), those who embrace Jesus will have His performance attributed to their account.

THE PRESCRIPTION FROM SCRIPTURE

Let's unpack this a little further by going back to Romans 4:24, where Paul says, "[Righteousness] will be credited to us who believe in Him who raised Jesus our Lord from the dead." In order for sinners like you and me to be declared righteous, we must believe in the person and work of Jesus Christ. He offered His perfect life in the place of sinners. If His life hadn't been perfectly obedient to God's commands, His sacrifice would benefit no one, not even Himself. Think about that for a moment. He had to have lived a life of absolute perfection. Perfection according to what, you ask? According to the very laws that God had set up for His covenant people to obey in totality.

Jesus said, "Be perfect, therefore, as your heavenly Father is perfect" (Matthew 5:48). We find this text in a sermon Jesus preached while at the Mount of Olives. This sermon is known as the Sermon on the Mount. The sermon shows Jesus' desire to correct all misconceptions Israel had about God's character and Word. Israel was being misled by self-righteous teachers who created a oppressive religious system that prevented people from having access to the truth of God's Word. These teachers made Judaism into a business for their own gain. But Jesus said that God the Father is perfect and that His perfection mandates that those who follow Him must also be perfect.

Let's look at a couple of words in this verse to gain a grasp on the depth of what Jesus was saying about God's character and the reputation of His people. The verb *to be* is written in the future tense (the action will take place in the future), middle voice (the subject of the verb performs the action), indicative mood (this is a command not a suggestion).[1] Jesus was speaking to those who are His disciples, giving them the command to be perfect as God the Father is perfect.

Jesus uses the word *perfect* twice to mean complete "moral perfection."[2] Since we're born tainted by sin, there's no humanly possible way that we will live perfectly. At the same time, since God is perfectly holy, He cannot lower His standard of perfection. Before we assume we're at a total loss, we must consider two truths that provide us comfort. First, Christ lived perfectly—and when we embrace Him as our Savior, He covers us in His righteousness (Isaiah 61:10). Second, since we're in Christ, we've been given His righteousness (1 Corinthians 1:30; Philippians 3:9)—yet because we're dwelling in a body that has been tainted by flesh, we must work in cooperation with God the Holy Spirit to put to death deeds of our body (or flesh).

New Testament scholar Eduard Schweizer ties all of this together by identifying a promise in Matthew 5:48: "Of course, the formulation, both in Greek and in Hebrew, includes the promise 'You will be' as well as the summons 'You must be.'"[3] Did you notice the promise *you will be*? The only way sinners can be perfect in the eyes of God is if they embrace the perfect life, substitutionary death, and resurrection of Jesus Christ. When Jesus becomes our Savior, in God's eyes we have already met His perfect standard because we're in Christ (Romans 8:1; 2 Corinthians 1:2, 21; 5:17; Ephesians 2:10; Colossians 3:3)—and Christ already met it for us.

However, this truth is not a license for us to be lazy in our faith and sinful in our actions. Theologian John Walvoord said, "While sinless perfection is impossible, godliness, in its biblical concept, is attainable."[4] Walvoord meant that in our own efforts we'll never be perfect; but because we're in Christ and He met God's perfect standard for us, and because God the Holy Spirit indwells us (Romans 8:9-13), we're able to live a life of pursuing holiness. But now that we have been given Christ's perfection, we shouldn't feel free to indulge in carnality; rather, we must adhere the words of pastor James Montgomery Boice, who said we're "to aim at Christ-like character."[5]

Since this is our reality, we must embrace what Scripture teaches regarding the sinless life of Christ. The Bible is clear: Jesus never faced defeat from sin. All four Gospel narratives highlight the fact that Jesus Christ never sinned during His earthly life and ministry. In addition, passages such as 2 Corinthians 5:21; Hebrews 4:15, 7:26; and 1 Peter 1:22 confirm that Jesus Christ is forever sinless. The greatest tangible proof of Jesus' perfection is His resurrection from the grave. Had He not been perfect, His payment, or ransom, for our sins wouldn't have been sufficient. He would have stayed in the grave. This is why Paul said that Jesus was "delivered up for our trespasses and raised for our justification" (Romans 4:25). What a powerful summary of Christ's work! The closing verse of Romans 4 packs so much punch that scholar Robert Mounce says, "God's entire redemptive plan is summarized in this final verse."[6]

When we embrace Jesus as Savior, we can place Him as the focal point of our most important relationship. If Christ puts us in a right relationship with God, He can heal our hearts from all the damage done by all our past broken relationships. Now knowing that the only performance that matters to God was the performance of Christ, we who have been saved by Christ can enjoy the freedom we have in Him by resting in His work. We no longer have to work to earn God's affection because it has been given to us through what He accomplished in our place.

Remember, a performance-driven life has one destination: the trap. The gospel message frees us from the trap, and the hope found in this one message gives us the courage and strength to take the Band-Aids off our bleeding wounds and allow God to pour His healing salve over them. Only once God heals our hearts are we able to forgive those who caused these initial wounds and at the same time see our fractured relationships become whole in Christ.

Chapter 3

AFFIRMATION

It's natural for us to desire affirmation. We love hearing words that express our value—and when we do not receive affirmation from those who mean the most to us, we feel a heavy pressure to perform. That's why affirmation is the third wall of the performance trap.

In *The 5 Love Languages*, Dr. Gary Chapman recognizes different ways people hear "I love you" through words, attitudes, and actions. *Words of affirmation* is the love language Chapman identifies that best relates to my heart. Throughout my life I've often felt like a failure when people like my dad, my wife, my peers, and my heroes in the faith withheld affirmation from me. I have also felt a double wound when someone withheld affirmation from me and then gave it to someone else. We'll further unpack that latter wound in chapter 4 when we deal with our peers, but for now I want us to work through the pressure we often feel when we are not encouraged by those who are closest to our hearts.

THE PRESSURE OF AFFIRMATION

Since God has created us to be relational beings, we allow those individuals with whom we have made the most rela- tional investments to become stakeholders in our heart. A stakeholder is a person who is of the utmost importance to us. They are the ones to whom we look for affirmation, encouragement, and fellowship. When we're hungry for a relationship, we will often easily give away stakeholder own- ership to the people who seem to want to be around us the most. The more time we spend conversing with someone, the more vulnerable we become, and simultaneously the stake they hold in our hearts grows stronger.

The risk with this is that if we are not wise about whom we allow to have stakeholder ownership of our hearts, we will endure the abuse of those who don't offer us stakeholder ownership of their hearts in return. Too frequently we allow people to have stakeholder ownership too quickly. When the relationship breaks apart, we are cut deeply because we were ready to permanently give our heart to someone who wanted to be in our life only temporarily. *Negativity* and *neglect* are the two primary causes of our hearts being broken and shattered by those we give stakeholder ownership to.

Negativity

We experience negativity when we do something that brings us joy and set our attention toward receiving affirmation from a stakeholder—and receive the opposite instead. We may pass a test, perform a task, play a great game, create a piece of art, finish a project, or deliver a sermon, and rather than receiving encouragement from a stakeholder, we receive criticism regarding how we can improve. There is nothing wrong with desiring positive affirmation from the stakeholders in our lives, as long as it doesn't control us or drive us to unhealthy performance. And this is the conflict we face: desiring to be valued and appreciated by stakeholders, yet taking it to heart when they provide us with negative feedback. Whatever response our stakeholders give us, we must make it bow to God's Word.

I face this conflict in ministry every day. I really struggle with negativity when it comes to preaching. My nervousness is rooted not in how people will receive the content of my message but in whether I am being diligent in rightly dividing the Word of God.

One way that I know that the Lord works through the ministry of preaching is by feedback from the people who have heard the message. Sometimes I've made a mistake in the pulpit, and people have lovingly come to correct me; with a joyful heart I have received their correction. Other times, people from various walks of life have heard the same sermon and all arrived at the same conclusion: They need Jesus. I value this feedback, but mostly I have an unceasing desire to hear specific encouragement and feedback from stakeholders in my life.

On one particular Sunday, three people from three different backgrounds came up to me after the service to express their joy about what they had heard from the Word of God that day. One person was an inner-city schoolteacher, another was a retiree, and the third was a recently saved ex–drug dealer. All three of them expressed the reality of God's grace in their lives, their need for Jesus, and a desire to study God's Word in greater depth. Although I was extremely encouraged by these conversations, the person I really wanted to hear feedback from was my wife.

On the ride home we discussed where we were going to eat, what tasks needed to be performed through the upcoming week, and who was coming over for dinner later that evening. After we settled the details of our upcoming week, silence descended on our car. In the very depth of my soul I desired to hear encouragement from my wife regarding the morning's delivery of God's Word, and with each passing moment of silence I grew fearful. I began to think to myself, *Did I make a mistake? Did I say something that was contrary to the intent of Scripture, or did I not clearly explain how to apply today's passage?*

Finally, when I couldn't stand the silence any longer, I asked my wife, "What did you think of today's service?" Elicia's initial response dealt with small talk she had with some of the visitors and members. I began to grow agitated, so I pressed a little harder: "How do you think the actual worship service went?" Elicia nonchalantly expressed her joy regarding the song selections and how she was blessed by hearing the congregation singing in unison to the Lord, as passionate about the hymns as the more contemporary pieces. By this point I assumed she was purposefully avoiding her assessment of the sermon, so I made up my mind to take the conversation to the point of no return. "What did you think of the sermon?" I asked.

Elicia, hearing obvious irritation in my voice, told me she sensed that people were connecting well with the content and that the Lord was working on the hearts of those sitting around her. Then she stopped talking altogether. I felt that she was holding back her personal feelings and that I had done something wrong. *What did I do that was so wrong?*

I thought nervously. Immediately I remembered the last time I asked Elicia for her personal thoughts and feelings about a sermon—and she responded by giving me three things I needed to work on. Needless to say, my heart was crushed when I heard no positive reinforcement or edifying words, only a critique on how I needed to improve in my delivery.

Later that evening I listened to a sermon by John Piper in which he expressed how often he felt the same way about not receiving encouragement about his preaching from his wife. I felt a little better. *If a great preacher like John Piper struggles with this, I must be in good company.* In his sermon he shared a story. He had asked his wife to imagine herself planning a meal for an entire week, only to have the guests arrive, partake in the meal, and leave, offering no commentary. Undoubtedly his wife would have taken offense if that scenario had played itself out in real life. Piper then told her that this was how he felt when, after he had worked hard to communicate God's Word to a congregation that included her, she provided no positive reinforcement.

After hearing this, I asked the Lord to prepare my heart to speak to my wife. As I began the conversation, Elicia listened before telling me that she didn't realize how I felt. She had just assumed that I normally hear only positive feedback all day and all week, and so she felt compelled to help keep me grounded by showing me a realistic perspective of what I can still work on to be a more effective communicator of God's Word. The conversation helped me to understand her point of view and her to understand mine. Since then we have worked together to find balance between affirmation and constructive criticism. Yet even though we have found balance, there are still times that I internally wrestle with those scars of negativity.

Inside the performance trap, negativity binds us in two ways. First, it causes us to fear asking our stakeholders their opinions because we assume that they're going to share more negativity. Second, it allows us to assume we're never going to be good enough to gain positive affirmation from our stakeholders. The performance trap now has us where it wants us: in isolated confinement, left to dwell only on thoughts that are contrary to God's Word.

Neglect

Sometimes there is no greater pain than being overlooked by the ones we love. We can put our hearts and souls into something and present it before people we want to impress—only to realize they barely took notice before moving on without comment. The pain of neglect, when not dealt with properly, can lead us in a never-ending search for attention from anyone who will give it to us. I've seen this countless times with young boys who have been neglected by their mothers and young girls by their fathers. Both groups seem to dive into relationships with the opposite gender too fast and too soon. They are overly willing to give their heart to the first person who will give them the attention that they always wanted from their parents. Sadly, the person who gives them attention isn't necessarily trustworthy—he or she can willfully or ignorantly end up manipulating and stringing along someone who is already hurting.

I've seen this in ministry as well. Individuals have been poured into by leaders, promised everything from being the leader's successor to having their own successful ministry, yet are never launched into ministry by those who ordained or discipled them. Time after time, I've witnessed people grow discontent from this form of neglect. Sometimes they get anxious to venture out on their own, and they seek partnership and support from anyone who will give it to them. Neglect will leverage our hearts to throw caution to the wind if we can gain and keep the attention of those we so desperately want it from.

One example of such behavior I've witnessed involves a group of young men who attended the same church. Each of them viewed their pastor as a father. All of them had a bad relationship, if any relationship, with their biological father and wanted affirmation from a male figure. Each of these young men had a desire to love their Lord, so it was natural for them to take their cues in life from the pastor of their church.

Over time, a couple of young men felt the pastor showed favoritism toward others, and their friendships began to fracture. Things came to a head one evening when one of the young men, whom others saw as the pastor's favorite, called me to vent about a fallout he had with the pastor. The young man and his friends had noticed some character inconsistencies in the pastor, and out of love, this young man decided to bring those inconsistencies to the pastor's attention. The pastor rejected the young man's assessment and began to question his loyalty toward him, the church, and even God. Things escalated and the young man left the pastor's office grieved.

I prayed with the young man and talked to him about the need to forgive the pastor and seek reconciliation while standing firm on Scripture regarding the areas of sin in the pastor's life. After a few weeks, the young man told me some of his friends noticed that his departure from the church left a vacancy for the role of *pastor's favorite*. In the young man's absence, they received more of the pastor's attention. Because they so desired affirmation from a father figure, they were willing to overlook the areas of sin in his life.

Negativity and neglect are real. Inside the performance trap they each form a shackle connected to chains of regret and bitterness. Experiencing negativity and neglect causes our hearts to assume that God treats us the same way. Our flesh feeds off this assumption; we assume God is regularly withholding love and affection because He's too busy correcting us and being mad at us. In addition, our flesh thrives off of the thought that God is overlooking us while pouring attention and affection on others because He loves them more. These thoughts couldn't be any further from the truth of Scripture.

THE PRESCRIPTION FROM SCRIPTURE

Our comfort regarding affirmation from God is nestled in Romans 5:1-2. Paul begins by saying, "Therefore, since we have been declared righteous by faith . . ." The word *therefore* points us back to Romans 4:25, where Paul informed us that the resurrection of Jesus Christ guarantees that believers will be declared righteous (*justified*). This is really a heavy truth that we need to take some time to unpack. Justified simply means to be declared not guilty by God. Those who are in Christ are declared to be not guilty of their sinful offenses to God, freed from any future charges of guilt the enemy attempts to bring up, and released from the spiritual debt they cannot pay, all at the moment they embrace Christ Jesus as their Savior by faith.

To give an illustration to this truth, allow me to walk you through a memory. My family and I were at a department store in Atlanta, buying clothes for the kids. My wife has the gift of persuasion when it comes to us tagging along with her while she shops. (Let me make it plain: She promised us dinner.) Of course, dinner would come after shopping, so the kids and I agreed to accompany my wife, the bargain hunter, to the clearance racks.

After an hour of shopping, we marched to the register with the clothes Elicia had carefully selected. We paid for them, received our receipt, took the bags off the counter, and headed out the door, ready to eat. But as we were walking out of the store and through the doors, the buzzer went off. Now, being an ex-thief I tend to get nervous when I walk through those merchandise detectors, even though I know I've paid for the merchandise that I'm carrying. My greatest fear had become a reality: The alarm went off while I was walking out with our bags—and I was with my children. I remember thinking at that moment, *This can't be real life.*

The security guard called out for our family to stay put. As he approached he asked for our permission to go through our bags. But throughout the entire time he was going through our bags, my family and I had peace; we knew we had a receipt showing that every item had already been paid for. When the security guard was finished I showed him our receipt. He smiled, thanked us, and let us go on our way. There was no crime committed. No one was arrested that day because our receipt was the evidence needed to prove our innocence. There is power in having a receipt.

For believers, our receipt is not a mere piece of paper printed out of a department-store cash register. Warren Wiersbe said it best: "The empty cross and the empty tomb are God's receipts telling us that the debt has been paid."[1] These receipts serve as reminders to the enemy of our soul and our flesh that Christ's work on our behalf is all that was necessary to save us. In Romans 8, Paul forthrightly declared that there is no condemnation—God will give a receipt to anyone who has embraced Christ as their Savior. No sinful charge against us will stick because we've been washed by the blood of Jesus!

The word *justified* that Paul used is written in the Greek passive voice, which means that "the subject is the receiver of the verbal action."[2] Every Christian passively received justification as a gift; it was not something we actively worked to earn. God actively justified us because we could never justify ourselves. We no longer have to fall into the performance trap of trying to work for a "not guilty" verdict. The moment we trusted in Christ to be our Savior, we were declared by God to be eternally not guilty. God chose not to neglect us even when our entire lives were saturated by sin. Instead, when we heard the gospel and trusted in Christ, He looked upon us, took notice, and declared us to be not guilty. What greater affirmation can we receive than that?

Continuing on, Paul said we now "have peace with God through our Lord Jesus Christ." The peace we have in Christ is a *fact*, not a *feeling* that fades over time. Inside the performance trap, we're prone to feel that failure removes peace between God and us. When this thought takes root in our minds, we can minimize the peace of God to a feeling because we no longer believe the fact. This thought is anti-Scripture and against the heart of our God.

The word *peace* carries the idea of ending a war and bringing together those two parties who were once fighting.[3] Because of sin, we were at war with God. This war is universal: It's between the only true and living God, who is completely perfect and holy, and every human being born since the fall of man. The spiritual state for every human outside of Christ is that they are born dead and into the slavery of sin (Psalm 51:5; 58:3; John 8:34; Colossians 2:13). But Paul told us that we who are in Christ are justified. And one of the realities of our justification is that we now have "peace with God through our Lord Jesus Christ." Jesus has ended the conflict between God and those sinful human beings who have embraced Him as their Lord and Savior.

Jesus is the only person qualified to give us peace with God. According to Isaiah 9:6-7 He is the *Prince of Peace*. The word *peace* also carries the implication of a relationship with perfect harmony that cannot be disrupted.[4] Since we know we have been justified and we have harmony with God through Christ, we can allow God's peace to rule in our hearts, knowing that our relationship with Him is perfectly protected. This feeling of protection, when realized, is called the "peace of God." In John 14:27 Jesus said, "Peace I leave with you. My peace I give to you. I do not give to you as the world gives. Your heart must not be troubled or fearful." The peace Jesus gives is unlike any superficial and temporal peace any person, place, possession, or position can give to calm our restless hearts. This truth was echoed through St. Augustine: "Thou awakest us to delight in Thy praise; for Thou madest us for Thyself, and our heart is restless, until it repose in Thee."[5] A more up-to-date way of saying this is, we'll be restless (without peace) until we find our rest in God.

While living in the performance trap, I personified restlessness. For years I thought peace with God was a feeling, not a fact. My heart was restless every waking moment of every day. When we're restless we literally cannot find rest, and the result is irritation. We lash out at those with whom we come in contact—mostly those in our own home, sadly. When we are restless we respond in a way that hurts those around us. We act like infants who do not know how to communicate their state of being or find contentment in a place of rest.

All three of my children have taught me this well. Each of them often reaches a point in their day when they grow very weary and tired. And everyone gains firsthand knowledge of their tiredness—due to their crankiness. My kids take cranky to the level of an art form (my wife affirms that they inherited their animated dramatics from me!).

To be honest, when my kids get in their cranky zone, I sometimes get to the point where I don't want to deal with them. On one such occasion, my family had traveled with me to a conference I was teaching at, and my young daughter Lola fell asleep backstage. After I was done preaching, Elicia asked me to pick Lola up off of the floor so we could head back to our hotel room. When I did, she woke startled and immediately frustrated. I tried to calm her down by explaining that we wanted to take her back to our hotel room so that she could get into her pajamas and sleep in a comfortable bed and not on the floor.

Lola began to scream and cry uncontrollably. I looked at Elicia as if she knew how to stop Lola, who was in the sweet spot of her state of distress. Elicia looked back at me as if I were the one who had the cure for our current situation. As I held Lola, I again informed her that we were walking to the hotel room so that she could go to sleep comfortably in a bed. Now, every parent in this moment would hope that their kid would obey with a heartfelt *thank you* before quietly and compliantly falling back to sleep. But Lola, now discontent with me for even talking to her, escalated into kicking her legs and screaming to be left alone.

At that moment I began to think, *People are going to assume that I'm kidnapping my own daughter or holding her against her will, or even being abusive toward her*. At the same time, Elicia and Izabelle, our oldest daughter, tried to sing a soothing song to Lola—to which Lola responded by screaming louder in an attempt to drown out their voices. Lola did not want to be talked to, held, or carried anywhere; she was restless and could not find comfort in her immediate surroundings. When we eventually made it up to the hotel room, Lola immediately fell asleep in the bed. When she woke up the next morning, somehow God in His grace had erased her episode of the previous night from her memory! Lola had no recollection of the way she had acted or the things that she had said, and she even laughed off the story when we told her what she had done.

I realized that to God, I must look a lot like Lola in those moments in life when I'm restless. But instead of kicking and screaming, I am prone to ignore God and not bring Him into the situation. I take it upon myself to try to create rest where I am and not where God is leading me.

Resting in Jesus means simply to cease from working to earn salvation and instead to trust what the Bible says about how God views me. I am in Christ even when I don't feel like I have peace with Him. As Christians, we fight a daily battle within our own minds regarding the peace we have with God in Christ. The world will try to make us believe that peace is a feeling and not a fact. The world will throw before us people who affirm us, possessions that make us feel like we are more important than we really are, and positions that make us feel as if we run the show sovereignly. But the feeling of peace that the world wants us to buy into has yet to leave anyone in the world's system fully satisfied. Scripture reminds us that having "peace with God" will provide us with the strength we need when we are not receiving affirmation from people, when we don't have the possessions the world offers, and when we don't have the position that we feel we are worthy of.

We must make the conscious decision every day to fight our fleshly belief that peace with God is a feeling and not a fact— and we need especially to do this when we are wrestling with the lack of affirmation in our lives.

Chapter 4

PEERS

The fourth and final wall in the performance trap deals with the perception we have of our peers. Too often we feel pressure to *compare* ourselves and *compete* with those who have been given greater levels of recognition for their work than we have and are often placed on pedestals by others. This pressure hides deep in the corners of our hearts, and we work overtime to keep it safely concealed. We're fearful of coming clean about it because of the potential of destroying our friendships. We assume our peers would reject us for the rest of our lives if they knew of our deep-rooted jealousy. Sometimes we want to keep our peers close so we can leverage their network of connections to expand our own, and if we make our jealousy known, we won't have access to their fan base. Jealousy will drive us to do the unthinkable.

THE DANGER OF COMPARISON

Too often in my relationships with my peers, I've compared myself to them even to the point where I have silently competed against them. In my unhealthy drive to be better than a hero in the faith, I have placed people on a pedestal they never wanted to be put on.

One honest example is the way I compared myself to William "Ambassador" Branch. His impact on my life began on Wednesday, November 26, 1997.

I had been walking with the Lord for about a year and a half and still struggled with listening to rappers whose lyrics were not edifying to my faith. I have always been drawn to lyricists who related to the streets and articulated their narratives with extensive vocabularies. The use of metaphors, similes, and complex rhyme schemes always triggered my ears and would challenge me to be a better lyricist. I constantly battled the desire to listen to rappers such as Common, KRS-One, Nas, Rakim, and the Wu Tang Clan. As a baby in the faith, I felt guilty for still listening to secular music—but I also felt that the options in Christian rap, while delivered with good hearts, couldn't reach the level of lyricism the world offered. At that time in my walk, the only two groups providing lyrics that edified my faith and stimulated my mind were GRITS and the Tunnel Rats. I listened to them both daily. Another rapper who connected with me more personally than these great lyricists was Tupac. Out of all the other rappers out there, I felt he was a voice for me and my generation. Naturally, when the Lord saved me, I looked for such a voice and had no clue that one would arrive on the scene during my senior year of high school. It was then that I discovered a CD titled *Heaven's Mentality* by a group called the Cross Movement.

Our youth group rented out the auditorium at VanHorn High School. In the back of the auditorium our youth ministry set up our merchandise table, where we could purchase everything from candy and CDs to clothing. A friend and fellow member of Set Apart, a rap group I was part of, bought *Heaven's Mentality* and asked if we could go to my mom's car and listen to it. We almost missed the service that night because we wanted to hear the entire CD. After that night, one emcee stood out to me from among the rest. He went by the name Ambassador.

The Ambassador's rhymes were not simple. They were complex, filled with witty punch lines and more theological truth than entire CDs of other Christian rappers. His delivery was confident, and his cadence, to me, positioned him head and shoulders above other rappers, both sacred and secular. I remember listening to the title track, "Heaven's Mentality," and thinking to myself, *This guy can give any rapper a run for their money*. Overnight, Ambassador became my hero not only in rap but more importantly in the faith.

Over the next few years I would become a more devout supporter of the Cross Movement, and I prayed that I would be given an opportunity to meet them one day. In 2002 my group, Set Apart, and I were blessed with the opportunity to open for the Cross Movement at our church. Providentially, this would actually be the last full show our group would do together. After the show I was able to meet the whole group for only a few minutes. Not much was exchanged beyond our names and a few words of encouragement.

A few years later, when I served as the youth pastor at a church plant, our team brought the Cross Movement in for our launch party. I reintroduced myself to the group and spent time taking Ambassador to the airport.

We had a total of forty-five minutes to get acclimated and share our personal philosophies on the state of hip-hop and the need for more Christ-centered rappers. He put a bug in my ear that day regarding his training in Bible college and how I should look into one in Kansas City. I asked him if we could keep in touch, and we exchanged numbers. My friend FLAME had recently signed with Cross Movement Records, and Ambassador encouraged me to stay close to FLAME, who was at that time enrolled at Missouri Baptist. I told him I would and I'd look forward to getting more time with him when God allowed.

As my friendship with FLAME, JR, NAB, and all our St. Louis family began to gain more depth, periodically I would hear stories of their time with Ambassador. They told me that his grade-point average was 4.0, and we talked about him as if he were Moses to our tribe of indigenous urbanites, utilizing rap music for God's glory. These conversations kindled my burning desire to go to Bible college while simultaneously fostering a level of idolatry of Ambassador. After I enrolled in Bible college, Ambassador's accomplishments served as my standard for my academic performance. I worked feverishly to match him—to the point that I felt I needed to also have a 4.0 grade-point average.

In August 2006 after a Cross Movement concert in south Kansas City, my wife and I were invited to eat dinner with the artists and the host church that brought them in. Ambassador sought me out and chose to sit by me so we could catch up. I was eager to tell him of my progress— I was two semesters away from finishing my bachelor's degree and, like him, had my sights on working toward a master's degree. When I told him I was looking toward enrolling in seminary, he challenged me to consider a ministry beyond rapping. After affirming my accomplishments, he once again changed my life by introducing me to a new challenge: urban church planting.

He talked about his philosophy of biblical ecclesiology and how it related to Christian hip hop not producing many disciples or healthy churches to follow up with the young people in our context. After I agreed with his assessment, he leaned over to me and said, "Damon, our movement needs more pastors and seminary professors than rappers. God has gifted you with the ability to bridge that gap for the pastoral side, not just for the rappers." This challenge to me came at a pivotal moment in my life when my wife and I were considering what seminary I should enroll in. Through our conversation he lifted my heart out of the ashes by showing me what he did at Dallas Theological Seminary and what he and his church planting team were planning to do in north Philadelphia. At that moment, I knew I would forever want to advance as far as I could in the world of Christian higher academia.

Knowing I had to finish my last year in Bible college strong, I took my studies to a new level—one that was dangerous. I didn't realize the lack of balance in my heart until I received my first grade that was less than an A+. The class was Dispensational Premillennialism, and I got a B-. Both God and my wife as my witnesses: When I was given my grade, I told Elicia I was done with Bible college and no longer wanted to be in the ministry. When she asked me what the real core issue was, I confessed to her that I believed anything less than a 4.0 was unacceptable because Ambassador never got anything less than an A+ in all of his classes. I praise God to this day for a loving wife who refused to let me cower out. She gently admonished me to take Ambassador off of the throne in my heart and put Jesus back in His rightful place.

Ambassador never asked or demanded to become the idol of my heart. None of my peers were conspiring with him to feed me stories that would convince me to put him there. He was there because I wanted him to be there. I wanted to compare and compete with him silently in my academic and personal pursuits. It wasn't until 2010 that I was able to tell him about the silent competition and borderline idolatry I felt, to which he responded by saying he was grieved that I would put him on such a pedestal.

In God's grace and through His sovereign plan, Ambassador and I have stayed in a good relationship throughout all these years. During his season of restoration due to a moral failure, I flew up to Philly to spend time encouraging him. It was the very least I could do after all he poured into me. When many abandoned him during this season, I expressed to him a desire to remain in fellowship, not only to see him restored but also to help me not end up where he was. I was sincere when I expressed to him the need for him to guide me away from where he was, and he gladly said he would.

As God would have it, during my first PhD seminar I was blessed to sit next to Ambassador during our seminar at Southeastern Baptist Theological Seminary. He's working toward his doctorate in preaching while I'm pursuing mine in applied theology with an emphasis in North American missions. During our week in class we connected most days for lunch and had great fellowship during our breaks. It amazes me how God has navigated my life: When I was seventeen years old, I was rocked by his rhymes, and at thirty-four, I was sitting next to him in class as we both worked on PhDs. Words can't express how much of a joy it's been for me to remain in fellowship with him after all these years and to finally have a heart that's not silently competing with him.

THE ABCS OF JEALOUSY

I learned two key lessons from my relationship with Ambassador. First, I always focused on where God was leading him while neglecting the place God had me in. I never appreciated where God had me because I was always looking at what Ambassador was doing and focusing on how I was not doing that and needed to catch up to him. I was setting myself up to meet a standard that was self made and not God given. Second, I grew discontent with the fact that God was not leading my family and me where He was leading others. At one point it seemed as if Philadelphia was the "mecca" of Christian rap and all roads were leading there for a permanent relocation. I tried to force our family to move there, just so we could be part of the conversation with the "in crowd." When God closed every door I tried to open, I grew upset that He *stuck* us in Kansas City. Elicia, through loving conversations, poured grace on my heart until I finally understood that God was not calling us to Philly because He had work for us to do in Kansas City.

While my relationship with Ambassador ultimately had a positive outcome, and still does to this day, much of how we relate to our peers may not always have such a happy ending. Too often, what happens when we compare and compete with our peers can be boiled down to three words: *anger*, *bitterness*, and *complaints*.

Anger

When we feel anger toward our peers, we can't even celebrate with them when God does great things in their lives. Anger emerges in those moments when God blesses them, and—instead of encouraging them and praising God with them—we feel that God has robbed us.

Occasionally I've seen anger manifest itself when a married couple who has been unable to conceive receives news that some of their peers are expecting their second child. The moment this praise report leaves the lips of their peers, anger begins to brew in the heart of one or both of the spouses, who feel that God has once again rejected them because He chose to bless others. They mask their anger with a smile, allowing "congratulations" and "praise God" to escape thoughtlessly from their tightened lips. But deep down they are upset with both God and now their friends who are expecting another child when they've been prevented from conceiving. Such issues are relationship landmines that the enemy of our soul loves to set off. If he can divide the body of Christ through internal disunity that passive-aggressively seeps out in our behavior, he can keep us distracted from our calling: to allow love to remain as our perfect bond of unity (Colossians 3:14).

Bitterness

When we fail to confess, address, or surrender our anger to the Lord, we're preparing the soil of our hearts to receive seeds of anger that will bring forth fruit. A seed of anger planted in the soil of a heart tilled by the hands of carnality is fertile ground for the fruit of bitterness. The fruit of bitterness temporarily satisfies our carnal appetite to hold a grudge. When given proper attention and nourishment, our grudge places a wedge in our relationship with the peer we were once angry with but now are bitter toward. When we see our peers, we don't know how long we'll be able to keep up our hypocrisy, smiling in their faces while feeling disgusted with them when they're gone. We try to keep our communication short and sweet because we're fearful that some of our bitterness will seep out into our facial expressions and interactions.

Complaints

Continuing to run its roots deep into the bowels of our soul, the bitterness begins to emerge during our time of prayer as complaints against our peers. Next, the complaining begins to overflow into conversations with other peers, while we never address our issues face-to-face with those we have the problem with. Our complaining can quickly take over our lives; we examine every tweet, Facebook post, and Instagram picture our peers put out on social media, hoping and looking for something that will show failure or immorality so that others will pull their support from them.

I've talked to people whose sleep patterns have been interrupted because their complaining, bitterness, and anger against a peer were so deeply rooted that it had gotten into their dreams. This is a dangerous place to be, and if we do not surrender these three things to God, our lives will slide down a slippery slope into isolation and misery.

THE PRESCRIPTION FROM SCRIPTURE

In my moments of despair over comparison and competition with my peers, Paul's words brought me comfort: "We have also obtained access through Him by faith into this grace in which we stand" (Romans 5:2).

Did you notice the personal pronoun *we*? This *we* is the entire body of Christ. No matter what blessings or position we may have, *we* all have equal access by faith into the same grace because of Jesus Christ. Understanding this frees us from viewing our brothers and sisters as the ones we're to compare ourselves to or compete with.

The word *access* means the ability to "approach someone,"[1] and the phrase *have also obtained* means "to hold in one's hand a possession."[2] These words describe having the credentials to enter a place not everyone can enter.

This idea of *access* reminds me of a time when I was blessed with an all-access backstage pass to Passion 2013. I will admit I felt a very high level of excitement because I had never before been to any of Passion's events, and that year their goal was to pack out the Georgia Dome with sixty thousand students. A few days before Passion kicked off, my wife and I packed up a large moving truck and, followed by our family and friends, drove two SUVs carrying all of our possessions from Kansas City to Atlanta. After our friends and family helped us unpack, they went back to Kansas City, and a day later was the first day of Passion 2013.

We were moving because I had been blessed with the new position of executive director of ReachLife ministries, the nonprofit arm of Reach Records. The Passion conference team invited Lecrae to do a concert promoting the new music off his most recent project *Gravity*, and since I was a part of the Reach family, Elicia and I were given tickets to Passion. As we were getting ready to go, she expressed to me her excitement about getting to possibly meet Chris Tomlin; his music ministry had blessed her immensely. Before we left the house, I received an e-mail with a special parking pass that would allow us into an exclusive entrance. In that same e-mail I was informed that our names were on a special guest list; we would be given credentials that said "all access."

Upon our arrival at the Georgia Dome, our parking pass granted us easy access to the special parking area, and Passion staff escorted us into the Georgia Dome. When we got to the door, we gave another set of security workers our names, and once they confirmed our identity, they gave us our credentials, saying, "You can go anywhere in the building with or without an escort because you have been given an all-access pass."

You've got to understand—nothing like this had ever happened to my wife and me. We're normally the ones who pay "high dollar" prices to sit in the nosebleed section of any event of this magnitude. The next three days were truly a blessing in more ways than one as we were allowed to pray with such men in the faith as Francis Chan, John Piper, Louis Giglio, and Chris Tomlin.

The one regrettable part of having an all-access pass to Passion 2013 was that it came with an expiration date.

The badges would not allow us unlimited access inside the Georgia Dome. I could not take my all-access pass to an Atlanta Falcons football game and expect to be allowed into the Dome to watch the game. Neither could I stroll up to the entrance of the Final Four when it was hosted in Atlanta and be allowed inside. As soon as the conference was over, our credentials were no longer any good.

I share this experience with you to highlight a blessing every saint in Christ possesses: an all-access pass into the presence of God. And this pass has no expiration date! Hebrews 4:16 encourages us to "approach the throne of grace with boldness, so that we may receive mercy and find grace to help us at the proper time." Let's be honest, no conference or concert greenroom compares to the throne room of God. As Paul put it, every believer—not just Christian artists, people who work for record labels, or conference speakers and their friends—has been given the right to fellowship with God intimately. Paul said so much when he used the little pronoun *we*. If you are in Christ, you are part of the *we*!

The reason we can be confident in the fact that there is no expiration date on this pass is because the words *have obtained* are written in the *perfect tense*.[3] This means a past action was completed, and the results of that completed action are just as strong currently as they were at the beginning. So when Christ died, was buried, and rose from the grave, the all-access pass into the presence of God was made ready and available for all those who would come to Him for salvation. So everyone—from the very first saints who put their trust in Jesus after His resurrection and ascension, to the most recent convert who just embraced Christ as Savior—has been given this access pass.

Paul also said, "Into this grace in which we stand" (Romans 5:2)—and this phrase is written in the *perfect tense* as well. Through this, we realize that what has been given to us is not just an all-access pass without an expiration date but also a permanent standing in the grace of God.

We really won't appreciate what has been given to us unless we contrast it with the reality of our former life before we were in Christ. In the beginning, Adam fell into sin and was separated from the only holy and righteous God (Genesis 3). After that, all humans were separated from God. We learn from Leviticus 16 that only on the day of atonement could the high priest enter into God's presence, and only after going through the specified rituals to ensure that he would not be struck dead immediately after crossing into the holy of holies. When Jesus proclaimed, "It is finished!" (John 19:30), the earth shook, the rocks split, and the veil of the Temple was torn (Matthew 27:51). Finally mercy had been set free. God's presence is now available to those who embrace the personal work of Jesus Christ.

When we feel jealous of our peers, our challenge is to reflect on the timeless truth of Hebrews 4:16. In those moments, we cannot forget the access that has been given to us! We must run to the Lord, emptying our jealousy before Him and asking for His forgiveness. When we're operating in our flesh, which prevents us from celebrating with our peers, we've got to make the conscious decision to go to the Lord and ask Him to help us remember Romans 8:9-15. This passage comforts us with the truth of God the Holy Spirit's ability to help us put to death the misdeeds of our flesh. After we have confessed our sinfulness to the Lord while in His presence, we must embrace the reality of forgiveness and repentance by changing the way we treat the peers whom we are angry with, hold bitterness against, and complain about.

As we walk in the freedom of grace with the Holy Spirit's help, we can celebrate with our peers and praise God for the great things He's doing in their lives, all while remaining content with His work in our own lives. Only then are we able to do what Paul commanded in the next sentence: "And we rejoice in the hope of the glory of God" (Romans 5:2). The word *rejoice* implies the ability to "brag about"[4] something. It's written in the *present tense*, which means it is an ongoing continual action. We're not to boast or brag about our accomplishments while tearing down the peers we're jealous of. Rather, we're to brag on our God, who provided all of His children with the great gift of salvation in Christ.

Since we have been given peace with God through Christ, we must have peace with those whom we were once jealous of. When we confess and repent of our jealousy and receive the strength of the Holy Spirit to no longer walk in a manner unworthy of the gospel, we will rejoice with our peers when God is working in their lives. Together with those in the body of Christ we can have joy in our future with God throughout our present seasons, storms, and sufferings.

A performance-driven life has one destination: the trap. We may look up one day and see the walls of **t**rajectory, **r**elationships, **a**ffirmation, and **p**eers closing in on us. But if we are walking in grace, we no longer find ourselves bowing to the pressure of performing for God's affection or the need to compare and compete with our peers. We are now free to rejoice in the hope of the glory that we share collectively, as the body of Christ, with our future with our Lord. The performance trap can only contain us as long as we're willing to remain trapped. As one who is in Christ but chose to spend seventeen years in the performance trap, I hope you decide to take my advice to heart. If you love Jesus, walk out of your cell and enjoy the freedom He has won for you.

THE TRAP OF GOD'S GRACE

TRUST

RECONCILIATION

AFFECTION

PARTNERSHIPS

Now that we've examined closely the walls that can surround us in the performance trap, it's time to dive into the hope we're offered in Christ. As we find freedom from the performance trap, we can be trapped instead by the grace of God. The trap of grace doesn't have walls, but rather boundaries that come with our newfound freedom in Christ. Boundaries are not bad—they provide us with balance. The boundaries in the trap of grace express the heart of Paul in Romans 6:18: "Having been freed from sin, you became slaves of righteousness" (NASB). Inside the trap of grace we're protected by Christ because it was His performance that was accepted by God, not ours.

We appreciate the freedom we have in Christ more when we see the framework of the boundaries in the trap of grace. Picture a fire inside a fireplace. The job of a fireplace is to contain a fire so that it can provide warmth and beauty. If the fire escapes the boundary set up from the fireplace, it goes from being something that is admired to something that is destructive, consuming everything in its path.

I want to once again make myself vulnerable to you as I navigate what my life looks like as I live every day trapped by God's grace, enjoying the freedom that comes with boundaries outside the performance trap. I want to be clear: The trap of God's grace is nothing like the performance trap, which is associated with a yoke of bondage to a works-based salvation. As we look at the trap of grace, we will unpack what being a slave to Christ looks like and how His relationship grants us sonship as fellow heirs to the throne of God.

The freedom that every believer has in Christ can be enjoyed in its fullness when we recognize the boundaries God has set up for us to enjoy our freedom in. As Paul put it in Romans 6:1-2, the freedom we have in Christ does not mean we have a license to sin as much as we want without any consequence. The freedom we have in Christ comes with the responsibility to live within the framework of the boundaries that God lovingly has set up for us.

Much like the performance trap's four walls, the trap of grace has four boundaries, also signified by the letters *TRAP*, each of which provides a direct antidote to the corresponding wall of the performance trap:

T: The first guideline is our *trust* in God. Instead of focusing on the nuances of where we think God is calling/leading us, we place our trust in His unfailing promises found in His Word.

R: The second guideline is our *reconciliation* to God through Christ alone. The pressure that we feel from performing to maintain relationships is no longer an issue because we now realize that the only performance God concerns Himself with is that of Christ Jesus, who offered Himself in the place of sinners as a sinless sacrifice.

A: The third guideline is God's *affection* for every single one of His children. It's liberating when we understand that God's love for us is unfailing and unconditional. This truth allows us to receive God's affection on an ongoing basis and to remain encouraged whether affirmation from others comes or not.

P: The fourth guideline is the *partnership* we operate in with our brothers and sisters in Christ. Once we begin to look at the Scriptures regarding God's work in our life through the stages of salvation (justification, sanctification, and glorification), we can understand that God is taking care of all of the saints equally during life's ups and downs.

Understanding the trap of God's grace provides all believers with the endurance to make it through our seasons of faith-ful labor and little fruit. This endurance frees us from compet-ing with or comparing ourselves to our peers because we have found a confidence in our Christ. This confidence allows us to stay focused, running in the lane that He designated for us indi-vidually.

God has created each and every one of us with the purpose of knowing Him. The Westminster Shorter Catechism reminds us that our chief end is to glorify God and enjoy Him forever.[1] Often where we fail as believers is both in seeking to glorify God and in taking time to enjoy Him. Life inside the performance trap doesn't see God as a loving Father but rather as an unmerciful taskmaster whipping us every time we take a break from performing. It is my prayer that your heart would be restored to seeing him once again as the Father who loves you with an unfailing love because you are His in Christ.

Life inside the trap of God's grace has allowed me to understand God's love for me in a way I never could have while I was living in the performance trap. When I began to employ the grace already provided to me to leave the performance trap, I uncovered a deeper comprehension of *who I am* in Christ. This understanding provided me with the courage necessary to surrender my struggles with self-induced legalism.

The best way I can explain the love of God is by telling you about the birth of my son, Damon Jr., aka *Duce*. A few hours after Duce was born, he awoke from his nap hungry, and as a result, he began to cry. While Elicia was preparing to nurse him, I held him in my arms. After only a few moments of being nestled securely between my left arm and my chest he began to quiet down. Elicia, needing to rest, asked me if I was okay holding him so she could go back to sleep; immediately I responded by mouthing the word *yes*. As Elicia fell back asleep, Duce looked up at me. Tears began to well up in my eyes. The world faded to the background as the reality of my deep affection for my son took center-stage.

I have this same affection for my two daughters. I loved them before they were born, when they were born, and every moment of every day since. As I stared down at my newborn son, I felt compelled to break the captivating silence in the room by quietly expressing words of affection to him. I assured him of my love for him and my desire for him to know God the way that I know Him, in an intimate way through Christ Jesus. I also took time to share with him my reasons for wanting him to grow in the freedom of God's grace and not be stuck in the performance trap as I had been.

Those initial few minutes of talking blurred into an hour before I realized Duce had not been awake for most of my talk. As he slept, content, in the darkness of our family's hospital room, I sensed that the Lord was illuminating my heart with yet another level of understanding of God's love for me. Immediately I realized that the only way Duce would gain greater levels of comprehension about my love for him was through my consistent presence. During his first few years of life, he'd hear the words "I love you" come out of my mouth—but he wouldn't truly grasp their meaning until he noticed my constant demonstration of what love looked like throughout his various seasons of life.

At this point I began to think through different life scenarios and told him how I would demonstrate love before, during, and after each of them. When he was hungry and frustrated because he was unable to feed himself yet, I would be there to give him nourishment to end his hunger and help his body grow. I would run to him if he fell and scraped his knee on the concrete, comforting him while cleaning his cut. If there comes a day when a girl breaks his heart, I will help him walk through it and come out strong, growing through the experience as God prepares him for biblical manhood.

I told him there may be times when he strikes out, fumbles the ball, misses the shot, colors outside the lines, breaks a drinking glass, puts a hole in the wall, or loses something of value to me; yet in all of those experiences, as challenging as they may be, I'm willing to walk moment by moment with him. My greatest goal in being a father is that as I am consistently present in the lives of my children, they will see God the Father's unfailing love for them all the more consistently. Our Father has demonstrated a perfect love for all of His children, beyond anything I could ever give to mine. I pray you grasp this truth while you're reading through this section of the book.

When the gospel frees us from the performance trap, we receive access to the trap of God's grace. Life inside the trap of God's grace provides saints with the encouragement needed to face the trials of life head on, all because we know our God has not abandoned us because His Spirit indwells us permanently (Romans 8:9-13; Ephesians 1:13-14). Life inside the trap of God's grace allows us to truly trust God because we have been reconciled to Him through Christ Jesus. And life inside the trap of God's grace assures us that we have unconditional affection from our God every moment of every day while He is preserving us for eternity with Him. It's time for you to walk into the destiny God has determined for your life: a freedom from the performance trap through the trap of His grace.

Chapter 5

TRUST IN GOD

So what is the antidote to stressing over our life's events and how they relate to our trajectory?

Trusting in God's plan for us for today.

The reason trusting in God provides us with freedom from the performance trap of trajectory is that His promises do not change even when our trajectory does. Our relationships fall apart, sports injuries sideline or end our career, family members we love pass away, we move from house to house or city to city, we start new schools and sometimes fail classes and have to repeat them, we no longer keep in touch with people we were once close to. Life is full of change, and most of the time we can't keep it from changing.

We must push through the valley of doubt that causes us to think that because life changes, God does too. This is an *untruth* we must work to *unlearn*. God is immutable, which means He is "unchanging in His nature and in His character."[1] He is the rock in the storm that cannot be moved by the force of any wind. He is the anchor of our soul that keeps us from drifting out into the sea of lostness. Every Christian can rest in the fact that God and His promises remain even when seasons, people, and circumstances change.

The truth that carries me through life's changes is the fact that I am no longer an enemy of God; rather, because of Christ I am a child of God. Being aware of this truth will allow us to trust in God. When we live with the conviction that He is immutable when things around us constantly change, we'll have joy before, during, and after every transition the Lord allows to come our way.

TRUSTING IN THE HARD TIMES

This truth becomes evident during those changes that bring about various forms of suffering. In Romans 5:3 Paul said, "We also rejoice in our afflictions." God is a perfect Father who loves His precious children. We should work to understand that we are no longer His enemies, and He never will pour His wrath on us; Christ already absorbed it completely by taking our place on the cross. When we understand this, we will be able to rejoice as we have confidence in Christ through seasons of afflictions. The word *affliction* describes "trouble that inflicts *distress*, *oppression, affliction, tribulation.*"[2] This word does not mean light sufferings or "inconveniences, but . . . real hardships"[3]— including those moments when you're being attacked on all sides and are scared to ask God, "What next?" because you know that some new trial or transition will come upon you after you've asked that very question.

Be encouraged: God has promised us that in those very moments, the afflictions of this life may squeeze us but will never crush us (2 Corinthians 4:8-9)! John MacArthur says that in these two verses, Paul used four "contrasting metaphors to show that his weakness did not cripple him, but actually strengthened him."[4] Those times when affliction seems to be coming from all sides are meant not to *break* us but to *build* us. This is why we look to James 1:2-4: "Consider it a great joy, my brothers, whenever you experience various trials, knowing that the testing of your faith produces endurance. But endurance must do its complete work, so that you may be mature and complete, lacking nothing." God promises that when we're in a season of seemingly never-ending trials, we can ask Him to provide us with wisdom on how we can navigate through the storm in order to come out strong!

I know it's hard to think through these truths while in the midst of a temporary storm, but take heart: All of your seasons of transition do serve an eternal purpose. Always remember, the best is yet to come. And while we're patiently waiting for it, we should reconcile our hope with the sobering truth that God never guarantees to disclose the answer to all of our questions. In this life, we may never hear His reply to "Why did this happen to me?" Knowing this, we should fix our eyes on the afflictions of Job—in Scripture, God never fully disclosed to Job about His conversation with Satan that prompted the evil one to challenge Job's fidelity to God.

At the same time I've learned to balance Job's story with Romans 8:28, which says, "We know that all things work together for the good of those who love God: those who are called according to His purpose." The challenge I often give to myself and other believers is, "What if the 'good' that God promises is never seen during this present life?" What if the answers will come only when we see the Lord face-to-face— does that give us the right not to rejoice in our present sufferings? Absolutely not!

Please understand: I'm quick to encourage you to make these practices a habit because I've had to do it in my own life time and time again. The most recent season of storms found my wife and me facing life-altering news last year. Elicia had been dealing with what she thought was a long battle with vertigo for a few weeks and finally decided to go see a doctor. The doctor suggested she see a neurologist regarding some concerns that showed up on her X-ray. Not thinking much about the referral, Elicia complied and had an MRI. Within a few weeks the neurologist called her in for an appointment. She had one of three diseases: lupus, Lyme disease, or multiple sclerosis. Utterly shocked, Elicia drove home that day not knowing how to handle this news. When she got home, she wept in my arms for what seemed like hours.

She was told she needed to have a spinal tap done to rule out all the diseases but one: multiple sclerosis. A few weeks later, as I was loading up the final pieces of luggage in our car so we could head to one of my speaking engagements in Memphis, we got the call that changed our lives. Her neurologist confirmed that Elicia was in the beginning stages of multiple sclerosis. Immediately our hearts stopped. We sat there staring into each other's eyes, completely unable to speak. After what seemed to be an eternity of silence, tears began to flow, and we held each other and cried.

Every emotion known to man rushed through my being. I felt like life was ending and I had lost my best friend. I was angry because I wished God would've given me this disease and spared the love of my life. I was scared because I didn't know if this disease would cripple and paralyze my wife. I was filled with anxiety because I wondered whether our kids would inherit it. If there was ever a time in life when I felt utterly helpless and hopeless, it was in this moment. Yet, to God's glory, while I was holding my wife, trying to console her, I began to pray out loud a prayer filled with Scripture and praises to God. Out of nowhere I began to thank Him for trusting us with this battle and expressed joy in the fact that He blessed us with this opportunity to grow in our faith together as husband and wife. In my lowest moment of weakness, God gave me strength. The Scriptures were once again proven true.

God has since provided Elicia and me with wisdom regarding the trials we face now that MS is part of our rhythm. A few weeks before her diagnosis, we agreed that God was calling our family to plant a church in Los Angeles. After her diagnosis, we found out that two of the best centers for MS research are in Los Angeles. If this wasn't enough, we looked at the climate in Los Angeles, and since there are many days when the sun shines brightly, Elicia will be able to get daily doses of Vitamin D without the humidity of the South! What a blessing—God knew of her diagnosis and even used what the enemy may have meant for bad to show us His goodness by confirming our call to LA.

TRUSTING FOR ENDURANCE

Scripture eases the tension in our souls by telling us we're guaranteed to grow in Christ while we *endure* through our afflictions. Paul drives home this point in Romans 5:3: "We know that affliction produces endurance." Now that we know that God promised we would never be crushed, we have to begin to understand that these times of suffering are guaranteed to produce endurance for this race called Christianity. The word *endurance* means "the ability to remain under difficulties without giving in."[5] God has given every believer the ability to keep running the race He's called us to. This all carries the idea of practicing and drilling the fundamentals of a craft or sport we've participated in—we need to build our stamina to the point that we won't tire when a performance or time of competition comes. All the training leads us to a point of testing that allows us to examine our ability to perform well and finish strong.

For me, this rang true every day before wrestling practice. My dad had a habit of arriving almost everywhere an hour early. Sometimes I think I operate out of a sense of rebellion to being on time because I was forced to show up early wherever I went while growing up. So what did I do with my extra hour of time before wrestling practice? I ran laps around the gym because my dad made me.

Now, I wouldn't run for the entire hour—just long enough to get tired. When my dad noticed my weariness he'd have me complete various stretches and calisthenics while my teammates were still showing up. When practice began everyone else was still stretching, but I was cooling down, preparing to endure our two-hour practice. This routine was my ritual from December to March, so naturally when the off-season came around I refused to work out or try to maintain any type of physical training in preparation for the next year. Most years I literally took off during the off-season. My dad would develop a workout plan and diet for me and set up summer-long training videos that introduced me to new moves—and naturally most summers I rebelled against these. When he would ask me if I was keeping up with the videos and my diet, I lied and said I was. Sadly, I was so burned out from wrestling that I never felt guilty about lying.

What I realized later on in life was that during those off-seasons when I would watch those videos and follow that workout plan, I always had successful seasons the following winter. Yet during those summers when I chose to slack off, my career suffered; my growth as an athlete was stunted because of my laziness. Over time, opponents I used to defeat with ease got better, and my margins of victory over them were smaller. By the time we all got to high school, I was struggling to beat opponents I used to pin without even breaking a sweat.

As believers, we are wrestling not against opponents made of flesh and blood but against spiritual forces of darkness (Ephesians 6:12). There is no off-season for us. Let me put it this way: We can slack off from reminding ourselves of the gospel while practicing our spiritual disciplines (reading and memorizing Scripture, praying, fasting, etc.) only when sin calls in sick. Since sin and temptation never sleep, take a day off, or call in sick, we must train ourselves to discipline our bodies and bring sin under control (1 Corinthians 9:27).

We've been given an opportunity to stay spiritually fit by practicing spiritual disciplines on a daily basis. Just as in wrestling, every day we compete against our flesh, the world, and the enemy of our soul. The competition gets more challenging while we are in a season of suffering, but our discipline coupled with the indwelling of God the Holy Spirit allows us to endure through our sufferings as we realize that Christ has already given us our victory. The endurance we obtain through our seasons of suffering and transition deepens our trust in God. As life transitions come and go, we who remain spiritually disciplined will stay grounded in our walk with Christ because of the high level of trust that we have in our unchanging God.

TRUSTING GOD'S PLAN FOR THE TRAJECTORY

I began to respond to transition in a way that was more pleasing to God and helpful to my family and friends when I stopped trying to force my life to follow the trajectory that others wanted. In doing this, my focus shifted away from building a platform and toward living to please God. I asked Him to fill my heart with a desire to run the lane He outlined for me—not for Francis Chan or for John MacArthur. I found that God often allowed me to go through the ringer before my family and church to expedite my maturity level of endurance in Christ. Each and every time I was in the pulpit, I kept my family and church aware of God's process of breaking me because I wanted all of us to grow together into one mature body (Ephesians 4:14-16). I no longer allowed the idol of individualism to rule in my heart regarding my life's trajectory because I was walking with interdependence in my local body, and our overall maturity was my life's focus. Sharing my life's struggles from the pulpit naturally drew vulnerability out of others.

When I made myself vulnerable to the congregation I was leading, I knew there was great risk. Yet I sensed that God's breaking of my pride would prove to encourage those I was leading. At the beginning of this process, I failed time and time again. Looking back, I'm now encouraged by the love and support my family and congregation poured on me during my times of failure. Without those dear brothers and sisters in my life, I would've collapsed and faded off into obscurity.

When I and a group of twenty people, which included some of my immediate family members, set out to plant Truth Bible

Fellowship, I was fully convinced that we were supposed to land in the historic Northeast community of Kansas City, Missouri. At a meeting in my brother and sister-in-law's back yard in late August 2008, I informed our group that I would find us a building in that neighborhood by the next Sunday so we could meet for corporate worship. The next Sunday, we were meeting in the Milestone Gym on 12th Street right in the heart of the historic Northeast. The night before our first service there was a murder on 11th Street, and during our first service there was a murder on 13th Street. We were in the middle of a war zone. I told our congregation that God wanted us to run to the place from which everyone else runs.

Over the course of the next two and a half years, our fellowship grew out of two facilities before landing in a building that we thought was the one God wanted for us. It was originally built as a Masonic lodge and in recent years had been converted into a church that had recently foreclosed. We signed a lease-to-own contract in January 2010 and remained focused on raising the money to buy the building outright. I prayed earnestly and sensed the Lord placing a plan in my heart to renovate the building by raising money to plant our church in the community He had called us to.

Sadly, within the first few months of being in the building we discovered flooding in the basement alongside an infestation of black mold that had been there for quite some time. Soon we became aware of other challenges we needed to address to bring the building up to code. Lacking money to make the necessary renovations and even rid the building of the black mold, I reached out to the landlord to see if we could get out of the contract.

Through a series of God's providences we moved locations and began meeting in the chapel of our mother church, Wornall Road Baptist, by January 2011. Two weeks prior to our first Sunday gathering at Wornall Road, I asked one of my fathers in the faith, Pastor John Mark Clifton, the pastor at Wornall Road, if we could meet for lunch. During our meeting at Niciey's Cafe off Troost Avenue, I poured my heart out regarding the current season of affliction I was trying to endure. I confessed my confusion: I deeply desired for our ministry to be rooted in the historic Northeast area. The building we were in was supposed to be converted into the community center to serve our mission field. But I was in the midst of a real fight with depression and doubt, as just a few weeks before, our landlord had indeed allowed us to be released from our contract and to vacate the building at no cost. I was convinced I had missed God and the result forced our church to leave not just our building but our mission field in the historic Northeast. I felt I was abandoning the trajectory God had set for our church.

With love, Pastor John Mark wept with me and counseled me to trust in the process God was working out on our behalf. He also shared encouraging stories of transitions in his own life that didn't make sense while he was in the midst of them— and he told me that after the dust settled in his new location, he realized God was with him through the entire process and was leading him to something else. At the same time we were transitioning out of the Northeast, we were in conversation with a struggling church in a different part of Kansas City that was in need of a pastor. After four months of meetings between both elder boards and congregations, both congregations voted overwhelmingly to merge, and Koinonia Bible Church was born in February 2011. On the first Sunday of March 2011, our church had a building to call its own, a new family we were married to, and a new neighborhood to have gospel-centered impact on.

Even after our merge I still possessed an unceasing grief for the historic Northeast and felt as if I had failed an entire community. Morning after morning during my time of private prayer, I would ask God to forgive me for leading our congregation on a wild goose chase after some romantic perspective on community transformation that would never be realized. It wasn't until April 2013 that I began to see God's work in the historic Northeast through our church's ministry. After moving to Atlanta, I began to connect with my dear brothers Dhati Lewis, Kevin Ezell, Lecrae, Matt Letourneau, Nehemiah Weaver, and John O. During one such time of connection with John O., while we were having coffee, I shared with him my sense of guilt and the shame that accompanied it daily. In order to entrust a new stakeholder with my whole heart, I also walked him through two other seasons of life that I felt were failures because of my leaving too soon. The first was my initial pastorate, which was a church revitalization ending in a split over racism, and the second was God's unexpected calling of our family away from Koinonia Bible Church to Atlanta only a year and a half after the church's birth.

John asked me to give him updated reports on the current situation of the first church I pastored, the spiritual climate of the historic Northeast, and how Koinonia Bible Church was doing without me. As I began to share God's great work in all three areas after my departure, he stopped me and said, "Damon, what you call failure, I call fruit bearing. In those three areas you were called to, you plowed, planted, and watered and saw little increase. Yet, in God's grace, after you left there now remains fruit-bearing crops where there was once only dry land."

His words of wisdom carved through the thick layer of depression like a Ginsu knife in the hands of a master chef. I had never taken the time to look at God's providence throughout my entire journey over the past six years from a different vantage point. That whole time I had confused planting, plowing, and watering with a lack of success, when in actuality God had allowed me to set up those He would call into those areas after He transitioned me into my next place.

I realized I had been playing the role of a fullback, a middle relief pitcher, and a sixth man during those years. In football the fullback often blocks for the running back. He runs through the defensive line to clear a path for the running back, who runs behind him with the ball to advance the team downfield. Most likely the running back, not the fullback, is the one who gets the glory, large contract, and notoriety. In baseball the middle relief pitcher is often called into the game to replace the starter who either got hurt or is not performing well. If the middle relief pitcher is successful, he will set up the closing pitcher to come in and save the game. Most often fans like to buy and wear the starting pitcher's and the closing pitcher's jerseys, but not the middle relief pitcher's. In basketball, the sixth man comes off the bench to allow the starter in his same role to have time to rest and recuperate before going back out to the game. Rarely will you ever find a sixth man in your fantasy basketball team's starting lineup.

Over the course of my initial four months in Atlanta, the Lord used Dhati, Kevin, Lecrae, Matt, Nehemiah, and John to help me arrive at the conclusion that I was operating with a wrong definition of success. I thought that success was measured by the amount of people attending my church and the financial budget that my ministry functioned on. After my conversation with John, I realized that success was *being faithful to what God called me to do while setting up those who came after me with an environment that is conducive for fruit bearing.* We can all be free from the pressure of our trajectory when we trust God in the midst of being faithful to His call.

Trusting in God does not mean that we will always know every detail about where He's leading us and how we will get there. Trusting in God means simply obeying His commands by maximizing every waking moment that we have during our days on this side of eternity. The chief command we have is making disciples, and this is a call that's never placed on hold.

Remember—God has given every believer the same job description: the great commission. We are all missionaries serving on the mission field we live in. God, who is omniscient (meaning He knows all), leads us to the areas He wants to serve. Matthew 9:38 records Jesus telling His disciples to pray for the Lord of the harvest to send out laborers. The language of this passage is similar to a relief pitcher being called into a game. Prior to the call, the pitcher is warming up in the bullpen, preparing for when the call comes to go into the game.

Right now you may just be warming up in the bullpen, making disciples who are connected to your local church. Don't grow weary in doing this—you're fulfilling your job description. Remain faithful until the Lord provides you with a call to a new assignment.

I have found that when God began to lead me toward a new assignment, I needed to pray regularly for Him to make my path clear. He then began to open doors He wanted me to walk through while slamming shut those He did not want me to walk through. The freedom that I enjoy in my walk with God allows me to see every day as an exciting opportunity to be led by Him even when I don't know where He is leading me. I no longer feel the pressure to follow a trajectory that other people say that I have to follow or even a romantic vision that I may have in my own heart that may never be realized in this life. That pressure has been replaced by a deep-rooted trust in the God who never changes even when my life circumstances do.

Chapter 6

RECONCILIATION WITH GOD

Inside the performance trap, the wall of relationships consists of feeling like we have to perform to maintain relationships—including our relationship with God. We think that if we don't perform well, the relationships will become broken. As we talked about earlier, sin separated all human beings from God, and our union with Him was severed when Adam fell in the Garden of Eden (Genesis 3:1-24).

But when we embraced Christ as Savior, we were given the ability to destroy this wall of the performance trap with the wrecking ball of *reconciliation*. The doctrine of reconciliation helps us understand that through Christ, we have an eternal right relationship with God. He who knew no sin became sin so that we could be reconciled to God through Him. The pressure of relationships is lifted once we realize we have a right relationship with God through Christ.

It's liberating to know that our relationship with God is not dependent on our performance. The perfect life of Jesus met all of God's expectations. Through the sacrifice of Jesus in the place of sinners, we receive the benefits of being fully known and fully loved by God. This right relationship with God provides us with the confidence to live righteously before Him.

RECONCILIATION IN SUFFERING

In a right relationship with God we receive encouragement that, as we endure through sufferings, God is still actively working in our lives every moment of every day. We can see the evidence of his work: As Paul says in Romans 5:4, "Endurance produces proven character." According to Robert Mounce, the word *character* refers to "that which has been proven by trial."[1] This word was often used to describe a precious metal like gold being put through the fire in order to burn out all of the impurities.[2] God, through the fire of trials, is purging from us the impurities of this world, allowing our faith in Him to be proven to be more pure and true.

A few years back, I would occasionally meet with a man who was struggling to find work. During our time together we'd share a meal while talking through issues of why he couldn't land a job. Over time, we focused more on lessons of biblical manhood and how God was developing him into a more mature man after God's heart. I would always make it a point to pick up the tab. I saw my time with him as an investment and never asked him to repay me for either my time or the tab.

One day he approached me more joyful than any other time we met, so I had to ask what made this occasion different. He told me he wanted to treat me to lunch in a couple of days. I knew he didn't have a job, so I candidly asked him how he was able to get money to take me out. He responded by saying that his mom had given him her jewelry; he contacted a local company known for taking jewelry, melting it down, and giving cash for the value of the precious metals that passed through their refining fire. He said that the envelope he mailed to them was large, and he was expecting a return of a few thousand dollars. I told him that if his story was true, I'd be humbled to accompany him to lunch on the following Tuesday as long as he took the rest of his money and worked to pay off some of the small outstanding debts he had. He agreed, and we put the lunch on our calendars.

Tuesday rolled around. I called him to make sure we were still on for lunch but was surprised when I was sent directly to his voicemail. I didn't think much of it, so I shot him a text, asking him to call me just to confirm that we were still to meet. I didn't hear from him by noon, so I decided to call him again. Again my call was immediately directed to his voice-mail. I thought, *Maybe he's busy or tied up and was unable to call, so I'll just continue my sermon prep and wait for his call.* A few hours later, he still had not called or responded to my text. This was not like him, so at this point I began to worry.

I reached out a few more times and still heard nothing. When I got home later that day, my wife and I prayed for the young man because she knew it was not like him to not return a phone call or a text. Later that night after we put the kids to bed, my phone started buzzing nonstop for at least one min-ute straight. Realizing the buzzes had no space in between them, I knew I was not being called but sent a lengthy text message. To my surprise it was from the man.

He expressed his apologies for not returning my phone calls or text messages and assured me that he was fine and safe at home. He then admitted he had turned off his phone that day out of embarrassment and guilt. His assumption of receiving a couple thousand dollars was jolted when he opened the envelope mailed back to him and saw only twenty dollars. He said he was able to keep only half of it because the other ten dollars was to go to his mom to pay for gas in her car. He told me he would call me first thing in the morning to explain what happened.

I assured him that everything was fine and said I wanted to take him out to lunch the next day to spend time with him.

At lunch, he told me that the majority of what his mother had given him was costume jewelry made up of fake gold and cubic zirconium look-a-like diamonds. When he called the company about his low cash return, they explained to him that although the jewelry looked real, only twenty dollars' worth of real gold passed through the fire. Everything else was consumed and turned into ash.

We will all face a similar assessment when we see Jesus face-to-face at His judgment seat (1 Corinthians 3:9-13; 2 Corinthians 5:10). All of our attitudes, deeds, and words will be brought to a place of evaluation before our Lord. All of the acts that we have committed in carnality will burn like wood, hay, and stubble, while all of the things that we did for the glory of God and the edification of His church will pass through as precious metals.

The character that God produces in us through our seasons of transition and suffering is not equivalent to fools gold or cubic zirconium. Rather, it is as gold purified and refined seven times as it passes through the fire of God's evaluation. Through those times of suffering we have been given opportunity to show that God is producing in us genuine character for His glory. As those who live in our house, fellowship with us in our church, or work with us notice this character, they will feel encouraged to respond in a similar way for the glory of God. This reality becomes tangible in the believer's life all because we've been reconciled to God through Christ, who provides us with all the strength we need to endure through suffering (Philippians 4:13).

RECONCILIATION THROUGH HOPE

In Romans 5:4, Paul writes that character also produces hope. Hope is not an uncertainty or a gamble—it is a guarantee. Biblical hope rests permanently in the trust that God will do what He has promised, allowing His children to anticipate the fulfillment of His promises. Biblical hope is not like the hope that the world offers, which is a *gamble* of circumstances. Our hope is found in the *guarantee* of Christ. But in the midst of our baggage from broken relationships, our view of hope is often skewed. We hoped that the relationship would not break, yet it still did.

My daughter Lola corrected my own skewed view of biblical hope. When she was younger, we placed her in a Mother's Day Out program in a church in Missouri that would give her a biblical education and time and space for interaction with kids her age. She began to thrive immediately. While Lola was at Mother's Day Out, I filled my days with meetings in various parts of the city, but I always ended my meetings by

2:00 p.m. so that I would arrive to pick up Lola on time no matter what part of the city I was in.

On one occasion, however, a meeting ran long. There was an accident on the freeway, and I was stuck in traffic—and my cell phone only had 2 percent of battery life left. I called my wife and informed her that I was going to be late in picking up Lola; she told me to call Mother's Day Out to make them aware. By the time I got off the phone with Elicia, I was down to 1 percent battery life! I had to go on the Internet to find the number to Mother's Day Out and had just enough time to call them, explain my situation, and make them aware of the fact that I was going to be very late in picking up Lola. The staff was very nice and told me that someone would remain with her until I came.

What I would later find out was that Lola's teachers and the staff at Mother's Day Out were more stressed out and concerned about my being late than Lola was. When the teacher told Lola I was going to be late, she shrugged it off and said, "That's okay. May I have a snack and watch a movie while I wait?" Her teacher was surprised at how well Lola was handling this. As my tardiness entered into the four o'clock hour, Lola's teachers once again told her that I was on my way. Lola simply asked for some juice to drink and another cartoon to watch.

Finally one of her teachers got up the nerve to ask her, "Lola, why are you not worried about your daddy running late?"

Lola responded, "Because my dad said he was going to pick me up, and I know he will. May I please have my juice now?"

When Lola saw me arrive, she picked up her backpack, threw her cup in the trash, told her teachers to have a good evening, and proceeded to walk toward me. "Daddy, what is Mommy making for dinner?" she asked. Amazed at her poise, I asked her teachers if she had responded this way throughout the duration of my delay, and they filled me in.

My daughter was so trusting in the fact that I would be there to pick her up. How often I fail to have that same trust in God in my own life! That day Lola showed me what it looks like to embrace hope in a person who won't let you down—even though, as a fallible human being, I can and do let her down. Biblical hope is that childlike faith in our heavenly Father who will never let us down, never leave us, and never forsake us. You can take every single one of His promises to the bank— none of His checks have ever bounced!

THE REALITY OF RECONCILIATION

The reality of reconciliation with God allows us to heal from all of the brokenness we've ever endured in every other relationship. Once a *right* relationship with God is a reality through the work of Christ, we can begin to forgive and heal from the wounds that we have carried in our hearts from all of our failed relationships. Because we have no pressure to perform to keep our reconciliation a reality with God, we can break down the wall of relationships in the performance trap and trust that God is working in our lives every moment, producing character through our trials. This character then produces hope, giving us further rest and assurance that our God will never abandon us or forget us. He's guaranteed to fulfill His word to us.

After resolving this reality with my heavenly Father, I was able to apply it to my relationship with my biological father. The Lord guided me through reconciling with my dad's abandonment during the state tournament so many years ago. As the Lord would have it, my mom and dad, through a series of circumstances, ended up moving in with my family and me. One morning my dad and I were at the table eating breakfast together. Prior to eating I'd had a wonderful time working through Romans 4–5 during my devotional time and had asked the Lord for an opportunity to put the Scriptures into practice that day. Little did I know that a conversation over two bowls of cereal would change the dynamic of my relationship with my dad for the rest of our lives.

While we were eating I felt led to open up the conversation that we had both tucked away for more than two decades.

I asked him if he remembered that state tournament. He immediately looked down at the floor. I pushed through the awkward silence and told him that internally I had forgiven him for what he had done but had never had the strength to speak to him directly about that painful experience. Today was the day, I told him, that we both needed freedom from that event, and I assured him that in my heart, he was already forgiven. I then began to share with him that my reaction to his abandonment was rooted in the fact that I was an unsaved, angry teenager and that since then I had come to Christ. The old Damon who cut his dad out of his heart that day was dead and would *never* return.

I went on to share how the Lord saved me and over time began to work with me regarding my unforgiveness toward him, truly pulling up bitterness by the root out of my heart and freeing me from the prison of unforgiveness. I told him that I forgave him for leaving me at the state tournament, destroying my fourth-place plaque, and then acting like nothing ever happened and never taking ownership of anything he did.

At this point something happened that I had never seen before: He began to weep uncontrollably. I asked him to look at me, but in his embarrassment, he refused. Placing my hand on his shoulder, I said, "Dad, will you please look at me? There's one more thing I need to say to you." Mustering all of his strength, he slowly lifted his head, which remained steady on top of his convulsing shoulders. His eyes remained squeezed together in an attempt to prevent more tears from falling. Seeing my dad's brokenness reminded me of his humanity and need for love and affirmation. As tears continued streaming down his face, I felt led to ask my dad to forgive me for the years I allowed bitterness to be a wedge in our relationship.

At this, he began wailing out loud. Within a few minutes he was able to gather himself, open his eyes, and tell me that he had waited for this moment for over twenty years. He began to describe how sorry he was for what he had done. In order to cope with the guilt he would consistently suppress it, choosing not to think about it and acting as if it had never happened. He begged for my forgiveness, and I assured him he already had it. He never needed to ask for it again. He reciprocated by saying he forgave me for the way that I had treated him during my teenage years. We hugged each other and cried together for the first time in the history of our relationship.

That moment would have never happened unless the Lord had primed my heart to understand the beauty of reconciliation through Christ. Many believers are leveraging bitterness as a wedge of separation between themselves and those who hurt them deeply—but freedom in Christ comes with the responsibility of reconciliation. If God has entrusted

His body with the ministry of reconciliation (2 Corinthians 5:11-21) through His forgiveness, how much more should we employ the same forgiveness for those who have offended and wounded us deeply? Although the pain I felt from my dad's abandonment ran deeply enough to alter our relationship for more than two decades, his offense doesn't begin to compare to the innumerable offenses that I have committed against God, who because of Christ was both willing and able to forgive me!

Now, we must also understand that reconciliation looks different in different situations. My relationship with my dad will have nuances different from how you respond to the person who may have molested you, or the person who broke your heart when you were dating, or the boss who racially discriminated against you. I don't know the context of your pain. Life after forgiveness will look different depending on the relationship. However, we may all operate under the general principle of walking in forgiveness (Matthew 6:14-15; Colossians 3:13).

Walking in forgiveness means that you will not slander that person anymore. You won't watch their every move on social media only to use it as leverage to drive your disdain for them deeper (Ephesians 4:31-32). Walking in forgiveness means no longer holding the offense against the offender (2 Corinthians 2:5-8). When negative thoughts and desires resurface in our hearts, we should quickly take them to the Lord in prayer and ask Him to fill us with love for that person (1 Corinthians 13:4-6).

When we walk in forgiveness we are no longer slaves to our offender and the offense they committed against us, and we do not have to return evil for evil toward them (1 Peter 3:9). We are showing both saints and sinners the expression of God's grace through the finished work of Christ. When we walk in forgiveness, we are giving a living and breathing example of what life looks like outside of the performance trap and inside the trap of God's grace.

Chapter 7

AFFECTION FROM GOD

Do you remember our discussion about the wall in the performance trap called affirmation? Affirmation is the pressure we feel to perform in order to receive encouragement from those we want to please. But when we begin to look at the reality of God's affection for us, we will be able to break down that wall of the performance trap and walk into a newfound freedom in Christ. Within the trap of God's grace, we can be free from the pressure we put on ourselves to receive affirmation from others because God's love and affection toward us is constant!

In Romans 5:5, Paul continued to build his argument about the love of God for His children by saying, "This hope will not disappoint us." The hope that God supplies us with allows us to see our growth and development in our walk with Christ. But we don't always notice the changes at first.

It's similar to our physical growth and development. I didn't notice changes in my own life until I looked at pictures from my past and realized I no longer looked the same. I wasn't the same height, my facial features had changed, and I'd put on a little weight since high school. I've seen the same process in the lives of my children. Since I'm with them every day, I don't really observe their growth until I look at the pictures we posted on Facebook a few years ago. Their growth is real, but it took me a while to notice it.

In the same way, we sometimes don't see the spiritual growth in others until they experience a season of heartache or suffering and their response allows us to see how much they've grown in Christ. In our own lives, we may think that we are still infants in our walk with Christ, but in His grace He has matured us and provided us with enough endurance to not respond sinfully to situations that would have ensnared us earlier on in our walk.

In 2 Corinthians 3:18 Paul says, "We all, with unveiled faces, are looking as in a mirror at the glory of the Lord and are being transformed into the same image from glory to glory; this is from the Lord who is the Spirit." Peter closes out his second epistle by saying, "Grow in the grace and knowledge of our Lord and Savior Jesus Christ. To Him be the glory both now and to the day of eternity. Amen." Throughout his entire letter Peter encourages believers to live responsibly while enjoying God's grace. To Peter, living responsibly includes utilizing the power God supplies us with to live holy (1:3-11), appreciating Scripture as being God's inspired Word that guides us through life (1:16-21), identifying false teachers and avoiding their teachings that lead to destruction (2:1-22), remaining assured of the Lord's coming judgment on the wicked (3:1-13), and standing firm in the knowledge of Jesus Christ to keep from being swept away by false teachers (3:14-18). Our growth in Christ is a process—it doesn't come all at once.

Yet even with these clear and encouraging truths, we still have struggles with sin. Throughout our walk with Christ we've made innumerable mistakes because we are fallen human beings. As I mentioned earlier in the book, I used to feel that I would never be good enough to receive the love of God. Every waking hour I felt a sense of guilt because I thought I was frustrating God with my lackluster performance. To deal with the guilt, I would either work tirelessly for God's affection, or I would shut down completely because I was tired of failing time and time again.

That mentality is fostered in the performance trap, but life inside the trap of God's grace is the opposite. In the trap of grace, we start to realize that whether we make mistakes or obey God perfectly, He still loves us the same. During our entire process of growing, He never removes one ounce of His affection from us!

Again, having children helped me understand on a finite level the Father's love for me. One time when I was sleeping in, my daughter Izabelle wanted to surprise Elicia and me with breakfast in bed. After she made toast and diced up fresh fruit, she pulled orange juice out of the refrigerator and attempted to pour it into small porcelain teacups.

When she tried pouring the juice into the teacups, somehow her hand slipped and she spilled the juice all over the kitchen table. The scurrying of little feet in the kitchen aroused my curiosity, and I rose out of bed to head downstairs. I found Izabelle hiding behind a mountain of soggy paper towels in the kitchen. I called out for her, and at first she didn't answer. Once again I called out for her by name, and this time all she did was begin to cry out loud.

I walked over to her and gave her a hug, which made her start crying harder! Befuddled, I asked her what was wrong. "I just wanted to surprise you by making breakfast for you," she said, "and I spilled the orange juice and made a mistake

and couldn't clean it up before you came into the kitchen."
Seeing that her heart was broken, I looked her in the eyes
and said, "Baby girl, it was just a mistake. Everything is fine.
Now, let's both clean up this mess." Her tears stopped as
I began to wipe them away. We cleaned up the mess and
enjoyed a nice meal together, just the two of us.

That moment will forever be etched in my mind because I
realized that this is how my loving heavenly Father responds
to me when I make an honest mistake or even blatantly dis-
obey Him. God's love for me does not increase when I do
right or decrease when I do wrong. As Jude informs us, those
who are "loved by God the Father" are being "kept by Jesus
Christ" (1:1). What a power-packed verse!

Jude wrote the two verbs *loved* and *kept* in the *perfect tense*
and *passive voice*.[1] This tense and voice assure us that at some
point in eternity past God began to love us, and His love for us
from that point throughout all of eternity has been and will
remain steady, unwavering, and unconditional. In addition,
because it is *passive*, I constantly receive His affection with
every breath that I breathe, and I do not have to work for it!

God articulates this liberating truth to His children throughout the New Testament. He loves us before, during, and after
we make our sinful and honest mistakes. And just like my
daughter when she heard me coming into the kitchen, we

naturally try to hide from our Father out of embarrassment when we make a mistake. Yet when we look at the reality of 1 John 1:8-10, we are confronted by the fact that because of the person and work of Jesus, we who have embraced Him as Savior can go to God directly and lay our sins before Him. He is both faithful and just to forgive us.

THE OCEAN IN A CUP

God does something remarkable to help us stay out of the performance trap. He provides us with the ability to know His love through personal experience. Paul wrote that we can know His love because it has "been poured out in our hearts" (Romans 5:5).

His love is unlimited. Imagine taking an empty drinking cup to the beach and throwing it into the ocean. Quickly the cup would be filled with ocean water. Because of its limited capacity, the cup can never contain the entirety of the ocean in itself; yet it is completely consumed by the ocean. Our hearts before we knew Christ were like that empty cup. At the moment of our conversion, our heart was not just filled to full capacity with the unconditional love of God but consumed by it. We will never be able to totally absorb all the love of God, and there will never be a shortage of God's affection for the believer.

The performance trap causes our hearts to focus on a lack of affirmation from others and to deny the constant affection given to us by our God. But when you begin to comprehend God's steady, consuming love, you will gather the strength necessary to knock down the wall of affirmation. Knowing and understanding God's affection will give you the strength and encouragement to live on-mission even when you are not receiving affirmation from others. Rather than living our lives for an audience of fallen people, we can live before an audience of One.

THE BALANCE

Now, if God is your primary source of affection, there's nothing wrong with responsibly allowing a few people to be stakeholders in your heart. In my life, those few have been my wife and the church leaders whom I serve alongside. Simply make sure that you don't neglect the unconditional affection from God and replace it with a desire to receive affirmation from your stakeholders.

I would challenge you to find stakeholders who know Christ as their Lord and will have a long-lasting impact on your life that fuels your walk with Christ to grow in maturity, not carnality. Safeguard your heart from allowing just any person access. I would suggest the following as a few general rules:

- If you are single, do not give stakeholder ownership of your heart to a person of the opposite sex. Making lifelong strides of intimacy with someone of the opposite sex who is not your spouse will only cause further damage to your heart as the relationship breaks apart.

- If you are married, your spouse should be your first and primary stakeholder. Together, the two of you can then decide on who should be the other stakeholders that hold you accountable. Do not give stakeholder ownership of your heart to a person of the opposite sex who is not your spouse.

- If you are in pastoral leadership, I suggest that your stakeholders be those on your leadership team who are of your gender.

I emphasize that pastors should have same-gender relationships regarding stakeholders because we all still wrestle with unredeemed humanity. During moments of weakness, we can allow our minds to justify inappropriate closeness and intimacy with a person of the opposite gender who is not our spouse. We quickly begin to make permanent intimate investments into a relationship that has a high probability of being temporary. When this relationship begins to dissolve, our permanent intimate investments don't dissolve with it. Many of us bear scars on our hearts to this day because we invested in temporary relationships, and we feel anger and bitterness toward those who we feel still hold a piece of our hearts today.

Another unique but realistic struggle in regard to stakeholder relationships that I must address is same-sex attraction. In our day the conversation of homosexuality and bisexuality within the church has become normative. If you struggled with same-sex attraction in your life prior to Christ, there might still be residue from it in your heart, and the enemy would love nothing more than to skew the relationship you have with the same gender into a sinful attraction. Again, because we all wrestle with unredeemed humanity, this struggle should be included in the conversation. Be proactive in setting up an accountability system that will help guard your heart from using good intentions as a doorway to create simple opportunities to gratify the flesh.

THE FREEDOM OF AFFECTION

The freedom every believer has in Christ provides an escape from the performance trap as it relates to fights with insecurity and depression because of lack of affirmation. As we begin to understand the unconditional affection God has for us, we will turn our eyes toward Jesus and receive His love. The lack of affirmation in our lives will fade as we live in the light of God's unconditional affection. Outside the performance trap, we can walk in the freedom of Christ, knowing that we are receiving God's affection with every breath we take.

Chapter 8

PARTNERSHIP WITH THE SAINTS OF GOD

Remember how in the performance trap, we view our peers as the ones we compare ourselves to and compete with? The freedom we have in Christ allows us to shed that former way of living so we can walk in partnership with our brothers and sisters in Christ.

One major problem plaguing the church today is individualism. The culture of our day marches to a tune of self-centeredness. Before coming to Christ, every believer was dead in sin and followed Satan without reservation (Ephesians 2:1-3). The moment we embraced Christ as Savior, we were transferred out of the kingdom of darkness and into the kingdom of light. We were no longer dead because God made us alive in Christ (Ephesians 2:4-10). The battle now is learning how to imitate Christ while shedding our former ways of darkness.

Daily we find ourselves in the fight of our lives against our culture. This culture tells us to throw people under the bus to make ourselves look better, while Christ did the opposite by making Himself of no reputation (Philippians 2:3-4). This culture tells us to use people and love the things they can give us, while Christ expressed His love for us by dying in our place on a cross while we were sinners (Romans 5:8). This culture says our world is cutthroat, no one can be trusted, and relationships come and go—yet followers of Christ should be willing to lay down their lives for their brothers and sisters in the faith (1 John 3:16).

There's a family bond we as believers share in Christ that should fuel our desire to work in Kingdom partnership together. When we're living Spirit-filled lives,[1] we won't look at our brothers and sisters in the faith as competition. Rather, we'll see them as partners in advancing the gospel message. We'll know we're seeing them in this light when we're able to rejoice with them when God is working in and through their lives instead of holding anger, bitterness, and complaints against them. And we step into the trap of grace when we understand that our peers who are in Christ will spend all of eternity with Him and us in the new heaven and new earth. If we engage with this truth on a day-to-day basis, we will begin to see our peers not as competition but as the people they truly are: fellow heirs with Christ.

As we discussed in the last chapter, the love of God has been poured not only into your heart but into the heart of every other believer in Christ as well. We all share this love, and when we realize this, it's easier to remove the competition toward our brothers and sisters in Christ from our hearts. How is this possible? God the Holy Spirit pours His love into our hearts (Romans 5:5). And the Holy Spirit lives inside every believer.

RESIDENCE

Romans 8:9-13 provides us with biblical evidence of God the Holy Spirit taking up residence in our hearts. Let's explore two illustrations to help unpack the beautiful truth of the Holy Spirit living inside of us and our need to make changes to reflect His residence in our heart.

Two Houses

Once, during my early years as a pastor, I made a house visit to a man who lived on 24th Street in Kansas City, Missouri. During the visit he and I sat on his front porch and spent a few hours working through life issues that were putting a strain on his interpersonal relationships. Toward the end of our conversation he had to briefly go back inside the house, leaving me outside on the porch by myself. I began to survey his neighborhood, trying to identify its rhythm. What I noticed was the difference between the houses that had people living in them and those that were vacant.

While I sat there in the middle of the hood on 24th Street, I counted four houses that people lived in and six houses that were vacant. The external condition of each of the ten houses bore immediate evidence of whether it was inhabited or not. The homes sitting vacant were boarded up, the local gang had tagged graffiti on them, the grass hadn't been mowed for months, and nothing but trash occupied the driveways. The homes that were inhabited all had signs of life in the front yard—toys, swing sets, weight benches, furniture. Each of those homes also had people visible inside; their front doors were open, giving me and all who passed by a glimpse into the rhythm of what was going on inside.

In addition, all of the inhabited homes needed some kind of maintenance. A few had roofs that needed to be replaced, while others had windows that had been shot out and covered with duct tape and cardboard. But no matter the condition, the houses that were inhabited all showed signs of life and activity.

As I looked around, I realized that every living person is like one of these houses. Some people are spiritually dead and separated from God. These individuals are like those abandoned houses where life is not present. Other people know Christ as their Savior and have the Holy Spirit living inside of them, and they bear tangible evidence of His residence. And just like those inhabited homes, these people need maintenance—the Holy Spirit's sanctifying work on a day-by-day basis.

The gospel helps us realize that we were once those abandoned houses. God sought us and purchased the deed with the blood of Christ Jesus! He did not see us just as a project to be flipped and sold; rather, He took up residence in the home that He purchased with the blood of Christ. Daily He is performing an extreme makeover both externally and internally of the homes that He has purchased. This is the reality of every single believer in Christ.

The performance trap would have us compare the work the Holy Spirit is performing in us with what He is doing in those who are our peers. We may notice that He has given them a new paint job, while He is choosing to strip our floors. We feel angst toward those who have more external beautification, assuming that our internal process of cleansing and refurbishing is less beautiful than what is seen externally. The trap of God's grace allows us to no longer look at His work in the lives of others as competition but rather to see it as an opportunity to give God praise for what He is doing in them while He is still working in and on us.

A Hotel Room versus a Home

Imagine the trouble I would get into if I attempted to perform an extreme makeover project on a hotel room that I'm staying in for a few nights. I decide to take out the bathtub, retile the area, and put in a stand-in shower with glass doors. I knock down a wall to expand the room, combining it with the room next to it. I figure it would also be good to upgrade the bed from a queen to a king size with a mahogany canopy for my wife and me to enjoy, and while I'm at it I'll build a balcony outside our window so that we can enjoy the view of the city.

Needless to say, I would be in serious legal and financial trouble if I changed the room like that. I have no right to take it upon myself to make those changes because I am contractually obligated to pay a specific amount of money to the hotel, which simply allows me to use the space for the agreed-upon timeline of my rental. If I wanted to stay additional nights I'd have to pay additional fees in order to maintain my presence in the room. The contract I signed prohibits me from making any changes to either the décor or the square footage of the room I am renting.

I would have to pay court fees in addition to the cost of the materials and contract work necessary to make the changes to the room that I took upon myself to make. Not to mention the cost associated with putting the room back intact, as it was when I first signed the contract to rent it for a few nights! It would be foolish of me to do something like this, because I have no ownership of the hotel room.

Yet if my wife and I decide to make similar changes in the home that we own in Kansas City, she and I would have the liberty (as our budget allowed) to do what we wanted. Making these types of changes would not classify me as a lawbreaker, because I am listed as the primary owner on the deed to the house. This deed gives me the freedom and responsibility to make those changes as I desire—simply because I own the home.

In a similar way, when God saves us and the Holy Spirit takes up residence in our hearts, He has full ownership of our heart and life. His name is on the deed because He purchased us in full with the blood of Christ (1 Corinthians 6:20; Ephesians 1:7; 1 Peter 1:18-19, 2:9; Revelation 5:9). He now reserves the right to make any renovations or upgrades He desires in our lives because we are His. All of the changes that He will make in our hearts and lives will show increasing evidence that He has bought us with the blood of Christ and now lives in us.

The challenge for believers in the performance trap is that, while we don't mind Christ buying us and blessing us with His indwelling presence, we get frustrated when He begins to make changes in our lives that are uncomfortable for our flesh. We want God to give us the benefits of His ownership while we control what He says and does as if He is just a hotel tenant staying there temporarily. The tension we wrestle with in regard to our peers is that we want our house to be a home—but we want to control it as if we own the hotel, and we want to limit His work in the lives of others by focusing His attention on us alone.

FIGHTING PERFORMANCE THROUGH PRAYER

As we allow God to do the transforming work He desires while cooperating with Him throughout the process, we move from seeing our peers as those whom we compare ourselves to and compete with to seeing them as those with whom we co-labor. While I was living in the performance trap, I consistently felt angst about the ministry "success" of brothers and sisters in the faith whom I love dearly. Now that I'm trapped by His grace, I've implemented practices that I use to help me not go back to the performance trap in the way I view my peers. Both of these practices are employed during my time in prayer with the Lord.

The Poison in My Heart

When I'm struggling with comparing myself to my peers, I begin to pray for God to remove the poison from my heart. How did this poison get into my heart? Silent competition with my peers drove me to say yes to every opportunity for ministry that came my way. I did this because I wanted my peers to take notice of my grind in ministry. I was too hardheaded during this season of life to realize saying *yes* to one thing automatically is a *no* to something else. Because my race to receive recognition from my peers caused me to have greater thirst for opportunity, I liberally drank from every cup offered to me. I laced each cup with small amounts of pride, and over the course of time, pride settled and fermented into poison.

When I confess my struggle to the Lord, His hands of mercy massage that issue out of my heart, not only during prayer but afterward. Because the Lord has already removed the poison of competition from my heart, I am able to rejoice when I see my peers affirmed by others or receiving opportunities to extend their platform in order to advance the gospel. The Lord then allows me to walk in this reality as I begin to privately and publicly affirm all of my brothers and sisters whom in the past I've been tempted to see as my competitors. If you find yourself struggling with ridding yourself of this poison in your heart, my challenge to you is this: Confess it to the Lord, love your brothers and sisters in Christ with all you have, and don't be so thirsty for opportunity that you drink from every cup handed to you. That's how you get poisoned.

Prayer for My Brothers and Sisters
The second practice I have learned to employ is that of regularly praying for my brothers and sisters in the faith. I have

found that the Lord often places one of my brothers or sisters in Christ on my heart so I can keep them lifted up in prayer. In the midst of this, I can't view them as competitors because my heart has been compelled to stand before our Lord on their behalf, interceding for their well-being. I now desire to partner with them in seeing their ministry thrive. At the bare minimum, my partnership should include prayer for them. When I have prayed for my peers and then reached out to them to make them aware that I had them covered in prayer, I'm often blessed to receive text messages and e-mails of thanks and appreciation, affirming that God placed them on my heart because they were going through a trying time.

FINDING VICTORY

When I became intentional about practicing these two disciplines in my time of prayer, God began to mature my heart. He has also helped safeguard me by bringing to my attention blind spots in my heart. Specifically speaking, I began to take God's grace for granted when it came to ministry opportunities. I felt as if any and all opportunities that were extended needed to have come to me and nobody else. This is a transparent truth that I have mixed feelings about revealing.

On one hand I'm thankful to be at a point in my walk with Christ that I can make myself vulnerable about this struggle. On the other hand I'm embarrassed to admit that this was a struggle while I was serving as a pastor. But I share this so that you may know that you are not alone in your own struggles and may see a way of victory in Christ.

My identity is now secured in Christ. It is no longer based upon whether I am receiving invitations or whether they go to others in regard to ministry. Living in the trap of God's grace gives me a desire to see more of my peers making great gospel advancements throughout our nation and world. This desire is now maturing into the rhythm of my life. Since I cannot say yes to every invitation to speak or teach, I now take joy in recommending brothers and sisters whom I know and trust for those opportunities. I have become a cheerleader for peers I once would've envied, and I now can honestly say that I enjoy holding the door for others as God calls them to walk into an opportunity in ministry.

God leveraged one particular situation to transform my thinking. I was given an invitation to speak at a large conference because a dear brother in the faith declined and recommended me to the team who invited him. This allowed me to see that the brother who recommended me did not view me as his competition but rather as an emerging ethnic minority leader who would benefit from such an opportunity. I didn't fully realize the impact this opportunity would have not only on me but on the denomination that extended the invitation. I was told that I was the first person of *color* in the history of this conference to exposit the Scriptures from the main stage, all because another man had laid down any sense of competition and encouraged me as a partner in the faith.

Being trapped by the grace of God has its privileges and responsibilities when it comes to how we respond to our peers and how we treat them and pray for them. I now desire to encourage and help others as they have done for me, and to pray for them regularly as they often have prayed for me. I praise God that I can now see my peers as co-heirs in Christ rather than as my competition in ministry.

UNFAILING LOVE

I can't think of a better way to close out this book than by talking about how deep the Father's love is for you. In the performance trap we believe that people show us love based on our performance, and because we desire to be loved we will continue to perform in order to keep them in our life. But in the trap of God's grace, His love for us is unconditional; it never fluctuates based on our obedience or disobedience. The latter reality is often hard to remember in the day-to-day because we are tempted to keep our eyes on the temporary rather than the eternal.

Whenever my heart grows weary through the storms of life, one passage serves as an anchor that keeps me from drifting away in the sea of doubt and unbelief. My flesh naturally wants to go back to the performance trap because it is a glutton for punishment. Yet my flesh is countered by the Holy Spirit, who indwells me, as well as by my inner man, who yearns to live in the freedom of the trap of God's grace through Christ Jesus. In that moment of war, Romans 5:6-8 provides me with arsenal to defeat the flesh through reminding me of God's unfailing love.

God's unfailing love stays with all of His children for the long haul. He loves us even when we are at our lowest. Paul said, "For while we were still helpless, at the appointed moment, Christ died for the ungodly" (Romans 5:6). The phrase *while we were still helpless* highlights the fact that we were dead in sin (Ephesians 2:1-3), completely unable to please God. Everything we did was tainted by sin because we were filthy sinners.

Imagine a person who has fallen in a mud puddle and dirtied their hands, their face, and all their clothes. If that person tried to wipe themselves clean, all they'd be doing would be smearing mud around their body. If someone handed them a clean change of clothes, those clothes would immediately be covered with the same filth. Unless someone were to come along and provide a way for that person to be cleansed from the filth, the person's every attempt to clean themselves would lead only to smearing around the filth attached to them.

This was our spiritual state before Christ. We are dead in sin and covered in filth. Any attempts to try to please God by cleaning ourselves up—whether through attending church, donating to charity, or trying to be upright citizens—would never cleanse us from the filth. Those things would simply allow us to deny our own filthiness as we fooled ourselves into thinking that we were righteous because of our acts of "righteousness."

The Lord, through the prophet Isaiah, addressed this very same topic centuries ago; He said our acts of righteousness are "like a polluted garment" (Isaiah 64:6). Isaiah was speaking to God's people, who were going through the motions of worship without hearts that truly loved God. The evidence of their lack of love was their constant unrepentant love affair with disobedience to God's commands. One commentator said that God was upset with "*every particular act* of theirs, even to their prayers and praises."[1] To put it another way, "In the best deeds of the best men there is some taint of evil."[2] Apart from God, all we do is sinful because our hearts our sinful. This is why "good works" do nothing to remove our sin debt. Scripture is clear: Only the shed blood of Christ can provide forgiveness for our sins and a ransom out of sin's slavery (Ephesians 1:7).

Looking back at our text in Romans, what Paul was communicating is that while we were still unable to do anything that was righteous—while our hearts were full of depravity (Jeremiah 17:9) and we were spiritually dead, in our lowest state of being—God took notice of our situation. God was not content to sit and watch while we were at our worst. Rather, He was proactive in saving us out of the depth of our own depravity. His decision to do so was "at the appointed moment"—God intervened at our highest moment of need. Salvation cannot truly be appreciated until we reach a point of complete desperation, when we cry out for help because we are completely exhausted from all the failed attempts to save ourselves.

What amazes me all the more about God's desire to save us is the fact that we willfully put ourselves in the position of needing to be saved because we pursued sin instead of a Savior. The grace of God leaves us more awestruck when we look at how we never considered God in our life's trajectory—but realize that at some point, God decided we were done running from His grace. And rather than punishing us by pouring out His wrath, which we rightfully deserve, He lovingly stepped in to sweep us off our feet, bathing us with a never-ending flow of affection. All of this took place while we were completely powerless to save ourselves and unable to wash ourselves clean.

Paul wrote that Christ "died for the ungodly." *Ungodly* refers to those who live a wicked lifestyle with no "regard for religious belief or practice"[3]—in essence, a practical athe-ist. One who lives a lifestyle that assumes God does not exist. Let's be honest: If we now follow Christ, at some point in each of our lives, we were ungodly! Our entire being was separated from God, who is completely holy, all because we personified unrighteousness and were therefore classified as ungodly. We lived our lives not considering our separation from God or the consequences for our life's decisions in light of eternity.

In my opinion, one of the most dangerous things we can do as believers is to live out syncretism. Syncretism is the inter-section of the *intention* to worship God with an ungodly mes-sage or method. Syncretism has been an issue with God's covenant people since the time He identified them as such by escorting them out of Egypt. As soon as Moses went to the mountaintop, the people God had just freed from slavery grew discontent. They knew they were supposed to worship YHWH alone, yet they were ignorant as to how to worship Him. So Aaron, having a heart to see God worshiped but not really knowing how to worship Him, merged the desire to worship God with methodologies that they learned in Egypt. And for a moment, the people believed they were doing well. But God exposed Moses to the reality of His anger toward the people, and Moses became an intercessor on their behalf, asking God to continue in His covenant-keeping love for them.

I wish I could say that syncretism was an issue of the past, but even today many people who claim to be in a covenant relationship with God fall victim to synching ungodly messages and methods with their worship to God. When we decide to remove the gospel message from our efforts to reach the lost and replace it with a message that informs sinners that they can work themselves into a right relationship with God, we've entered into the dangerous world of syncretism. These individuals, when left to their own reasoning, live under the assumption that—even though they have never embraced Christ as Savior—they are already in a relationship with a God who is pleased with them . . . while according to Scripture, they are living in unrepentant disobedience.

Yet where there is life, there is hope, and Paul's words regarding Christ dying for the ungodly ring louder than ever before in the face of syncretism. The call to salvation is heard through the foolishness of preaching the gospel (1 Corinthians 1:18-21). Through the gospel proclamation of Christians, God the Father draws sinners to Christ for salvation (John 6:44; Romans 1:16-17; 10:9-17). The reason the Cross remains central to our faith is because it's the symbol of God's unfailing love toward human beings while we were at our lowest point.

Just as a ray of sunshine looks all the more beautiful when it is contrasted with dark stormy clouds, the love of God shines brightly against the darkness of human depravity. The fallen world that we live in increasingly is getting worse. Decades ago sins that were hidden well are now done without shame in the public eye. Expressing biblical convictions is rejected in the court of popular opinion. Abstaining from sexual immorality until marriage, which is biblically identified as a lifelong covenant between one man and one woman, is now seen as archaic and even detestable. The Word of God has been watered down and diluted to the point that it is almost nonexistent in many sermons heard in churches and on TV today.

Rather than throwing our hands up and crying out for God to hit the reset button and take us all back to the Garden of Eden, believers must face the reality that the gospel is seen in a better light when it's contrasted against the landscape of present-day darkness. Christianity was born in a social climate that was anti-God! The evidence for the darkness of humanity came fifty days prior to the birthday of the church, when Christ surrendered His life as a ransom in the place of sinners (Mark 10:45). Throughout the church's infancy, Christians were socially pigeonholed as "cannibals,"[4] and Roman emperors outlawed our very faith during the first two centuries of its existence.[5]

During the first century, the gospel began to successfully push back the darkness that surrounded it—through the agency of disciple-making Christians. But throughout the course of church history, darkness has remained a constant backdrop to the gospel. In our present day, whether it is through the unjust incarceration of Pastor Saeed Abedini[6] or the murder of Christian brothers and sisters by the guns of Boko Haram,[7] the message of the gospel marches on through the members of the body of Christ who are still God's work-in-progress. God works in spite of us, not because of us, and the evidence of this is seen through the unfailing love He distributes to His children.

For this reason, Paul continued, "For rarely will someone die for a just person—though for a good person perhaps someone might even dare to die" (Romans 5:7). Imagine that a person who sold drugs, broke into homes, and terrorized people by assaulting them eventually murdered someone close to you. If that person was caught and prosecuted and found guilty, is there any chance you would ask the judge to let you take upon yourself the death sentence by lethal injection? If you're honest, you would say slim to none at best. No one wants to die for an ungodly person. Yet what about an upstanding citizen with a brilliant mind, someone who could discover the cure for cancer—do you think you would die for them? If not you, some other person might be willing to give up their life to save the person who could potentially cure cancer, right?

This is why Paul said it's a rarity for anybody to volunteer to die for a righteous person (who may be classified as a good citizen who pays their taxes, drives under the speed limit, and takes care of their lawn), though maybe somebody might die for a good person—someone who contributes many good things to the world. But everybody universally agrees that they would never die for an ungodly person.

Paul, though, came to a powerful conclusion in Romans 5:8: "But God proves His own love for us in that while we were still sinners, Christ died for us!" Arguably two of the most powerful words in all of Scripture open this verse: *but God*. Paul used these words intentionally to contrast the sinful, completely hopeless and helpless state of humanity with the unfailing love of God.

It was while we were in our hopeless condition that God actively chose to show His love for us, being proactive instead of reactive. His love was not just in word alone—it was in the very action of God on the cross. The sacrifice of Jesus was one of a substitution: He stood in our place, the place of the rightful people who were supposed to be there. The sin of God's people was nailed to that cross, and through the shed blood of our Savior, those sins are completely erased for all of eternity.

God looked at us in our low estate and demonstrated His love by dying for us, and He loves us the same now! He will always have this unfailing love for us. Receiving this love comes with the responsibility of distributing it freely to others as it was freely given to us. We get it wrong by withholding the unfailing love of God from those who fail us. When we choose to hold onto bitterness rather than releasing forgiveness or relinquishing consequences, we are neglecting the reality of the Cross.

Don't force others into the performance trap that Christ has freed you from. If you understand freedom in Christ, give it out to everyone you come in contact with. When Christians do this, we are living truly countercultural lives, contrasting the darkness of our fallen world with the marvelous light of the message of the gospel of Christ.

Look around you: This dark world is inhabited by people who not only love darkness but are content remaining in it! Masses of people on this planet are running from the message of the Cross because the life of Christ exposes the guilt and shame of their indwelling sin. When you look at them, don't see them as people you must run from; see them as those you are to run to. If you won't go to them and share the powerful life-altering message of the gospel, then who will (Romans 10:14-15)?

The world around you is filled with people who turn to various forms of religion, materialism, and masks to hide their insecurities, trying to alleviate the symptoms of the disease of sin. They're in dire need of believers who are walking with Christ to share with them the unfailing love of God, who demonstrated His love for sinners while we were in our state of sinfulness. No other message outside of the gospel provides resurrection to the dead sinner. The same gospel message that was proclaimed in Scripture is needed for our world today. The gospel needs no upgrades. It is the power of God encapsulated into one message.

In addition, those who are in Christ but are not living in the freedom of Christ through the trap of God's grace are in need of your timely counsel. Show them the way out of the performance trap. God has put believers together in community. We bear the corporate responsibility to see converts become disciples and believers transition from milk to meat, and together in community we can actively advance the gospel. People in your small groups, Sunday school classes, youth groups, campus ministries, and church plants may seem as though they are simply busy in ministry, but they may in fact be tenaciously working for the affection of God.

Imagine the freedom they will have as you share God's work through your life story and how you left the performance trap in order to find rest in Christ. Show them the trap of His grace. Your Savior has commissioned you to go into the entire world and make disciples from all ethnicities who will then disciple others. I can think of no better way to see the church advance in her commission than to watch believers enjoy freedom in the trap of God's grace and to multiply that freedom across the world. Imagine how far we could push back the darkness if we walked every moment of our day in full confidence of the unfailing love of God through the trap of His grace. Go and walk in the freedom given to you by your Savior Jesus!

NOTES

INTRODUCTION
1. *The Oxford English Dictionary*, s.v. "performance."
2. Richard J. Krejcir, "Statistics on Pastors: What Is Going On with the Pastors in America?" *Into Thy Word*, http://www.intothyword.org /apps/articles/?articleid=36562. Accessed on June 5, 2015.
3. Jennifer LeClaire, "Why Are So Many Pastors Committing Suicide?" *Charisma News*, December 11, 2013, http://www.charismanews.com /opinion/watchman-on-the-wall/42063-why-are-so-many-pastors -committing-suicide. Accessed on September 23, 2015.
4. John Piper, "Oh, That I May Never Loiter on My Heavenly Journey! Reflections on the Life and Ministry of David Brainerd," *Desiring God* (blog), January 31, 1990, http://www.desiringgod.org/messages/oh -that-i-may-never-loiter-on-my-heavenly-journey. Accessed on June 5, 2015.

CHAPTER 1: TRAJECTORY
1. C. K. Barrett, *The First Epistle to the Corinthians* (London: Continuum, 1968), 286.

2. Gordon Fee, *The First Epistle to the Corinthians* (Grand Rapids: Eerdmans, 1987), 657.
3. Robert Wilkin, ed., *The Grace New Testament Commentary* (Denton, TX: Grace Evangelical Society, 2010), 753.
4. Thomas Constable, "Notes on 1 Corinthians," http://www.soniclight .com/constable/notes/pdf/1corinthians.pdf, 167. Accessed on January 27, 2015. Italics added.
5. Horst Balz and Gerhard Schneider, *Exegetical Dictionary of the New Testament* (Grand Rapids: Eerdmans, 1990), 354.
6. William Arndt, Frederick W. Danker, and Walter Bauer, *A Greek-English Lexicon of the New Testament and Other Early Christian Literature* (Chicago: University of Chicago Press, 2000), 1039.

CHAPTER 2: RELATIONSHIPS

1. Albert L. Lukaszewski, Mark Dubis, and J. Ted Blakley. *The Lexham Syntactic Greek New Testament, SBL Edition: Expansions and Annotations* (Bellingham, WA: Lexham Press, 2011).
2. James Swanson, *Dictionary of Biblical Languages with Semantic Domains: Greek (New Testament)*, vol. 8 (Oak Harbor: Logos Research Systems, Inc., 1997), 67.
3. Eduard Schweizer, *The Good News According to Matthew* (Louisville, KY: John Knox Press, 1975), 135.
4. John F. Walvoord, *Matthew: Thy Kingdom Come* (Grand Rapids: Kregel, 1974), 51.
5. James Montgomery Boice, *The Gospel of Matthew* (Grand Rapids: Baker Books, 2001), 94.
6. Robert Mounce, *The New American Commentary: Romans*, vol. 27 (Nashville: Broadman & Holman Publishers, 1995), 131.

CHAPTER 3: AFFIRMATION

1. Warren Wiersbe, *Be Transformed (John 13–21): Christ's Triumph Means Your Transformation* (Colorado Springs: David C. Cook, 1986), 119.
2. Michael Heiser and Vincent M. Setterholm, *Glossary of Morpho-Syntactic Database Terminology* (Bellingham, WA: Lexham Press, 2013).
3. Ceslas Spicq and James D. Ernest, *Theological Lexicon of the New Testament*, vol. 1 (Peabody, MA: Hendrickson Publishers, 1994), 425–426.
4. Jonathon Lookadoo, "Peace," *Lexham Theological Wordbook*, ed. Douglas Mangum, Derek R. Brown, Rachel Klippenstein, and Rebekah Hurst (Bellingham, WA: Lexham Press, 2014).

5. Saint Augustine, *The Confessions of St. Augustine*, ed. Temple Scott (New York: E. P. Dutton & Company, 1900), 5.

CHAPTER 4: PEERS
1. William Arndt, Frederick W. Danker, and Walter Bauer, *A Greek-English Lexicon of the New Testament and Other Early Christian Literature* (Chicago: University of Chicago Press, 2000), 876.
2. Johannes Louw and Eugene Albert Nida, *Greek-English Lexicon of the New Testament: Based on Semantic Domains*, vol. 1 (New York: United Bible Societies, 1996), 557.
3. Michael Heiser and Vincent M. Setterholm, *Glossary of Morpho-Syntactic Database Terminology* (Bellingham, WA: Lexham Press, 2013).
4. James Swanson, *Dictionary of Biblical Languages with Semantic Domains: Greek (New Testament)*, vol. 3 (Oak Harbor: Logos Research Systems, Inc., 1997), 645.

PART 2: THE TRAP OF GOD'S GRACE
1. "The Westminster Shorter Catechism," The Orthodox Presbyterian Church, http://www.opc.org/sc.html. Accessed on June 2, 2015.

CHAPTER 5: TRUST IN GOD
1. *Holman Illustrated Bible Dictionary*, Chad Brand, Charles Draper, Archie England et. al., eds. (Nashville: Holman Bible Publishers, 2003), 810.
2. Walter Arndt, F. W. Danker, Walter Bauer, *A Greek-English Lexicon of the New Testament and Other Early Christian Literature* (Chicago: University of Chicago Press, 2000), 457. Italics in original.
3. Leon Morris, *The Epistle to the Romans* (Grand Rapids: Eerdmans, 1988), 220.
4. John MacArthur, *The MacArthur Study Bible* (Nashville: Thomas Nelson, 1997), 1796.
5. John F. Walvoord and Roy B. Zuck, *The Bible Knowledge Commentary: An Exposition of the Scriptures*, vol. 2 (Wheaton, IL: Victor Books, 1985), 456.

CHAPTER 6: RECONCILIATION WITH GOD
1. Robert Mounce, *The New American Commentary: Romans*, vol. 27 (Nashville: Broadman & Holman Publishers, 1995), 135.
2. William Barclay, *The Letter to the Romans* (Louisville, KY: Westminster John Knox Press, 1975), 87.

CHAPTER 7: AFFECTION FROM GOD

1. Michael Heiser and Vincent M. Setterholm, *Glossary of Morpho-Syntactic Database Terminology* (Bellingham, WA: Lexham Press, 2013).

CHAPTER 8: PARTNERSHIPS WITH THE SAINTS OF GOD

1. I define being Spirit-filled as daily abiding in constant fellowship with God (John 15:1-11), allowing God's Word to be the *referee or umpire* of our actions (Colossians 3:15-17), submitting to the Holy Spirit's control (Ephesians 5:18) so He can bear His fruit through us (Galatians 5:22-23), and confessing our sins (1 John 1:8-10). When elements naturally form the rhythm of our life, we're bearing the evidence of God the Holy Spirit influencing us.

EPILOGUE: UNFAILING LOVE

1. Robert Jamieson, A. R. Fausset, and David Brown, *Commentary Critical and Explanatory on the Whole Bible*, vol. 1 (Oak Harbor, WA: Logos Research Systems, Inc., 1997), 501.
2. Henry D. M. Spence-Jones, ed., *The Pulpit Commentary: Isaiah*, vol. 2 (New York: Funk & Wagnalls Company, 1910), 460.
3. James Swanson, *Dictionary of Biblical Languages with Semantic Domains: Greek (New Testament)*, vol. 7 (Oak Harbor, WA: Logos Research Systems, Inc., 1997), 185.
4. F. L. Cross and Elizabeth A. Livingstone, eds., *The Oxford Dictionary of the Christian Church* (Oxford: Oxford University Press, 2005), 1266.
5. John Barry, Lazarus Wentz, Douglas Mangum, et. al., eds., *The Lexham Bible Dictionary* (Bellingham, WA: Lexham Press, 2012, 2013, 2014).
6. Jordan Sekulow, "Saeed's Heartbreaking Christmas Letter," ACLJ, December 15, 2014, http://aclj.org/persecuted-church/american -pastor-saeed-writes-heartwarming-christmas-letter-from-hard -cold-prison. Accessed on February 2, 2015.
7. Stoyan Zaimov, "2,000 Killed by Boko Haram, Corpses 'Strewn on Streets,' Churches Burned," *Christian Post*, January 9, 2015, http:// www.christianpost.com/news/2000-killed-by-boko-haram-corpses -strewn-on-streets-churches-burned-132349. Accessed on February 2, 2015.

ABOUT THE AUTHOR

D. A. Horton is currently planting a church in Los Angeles. He served as the national coordinator of Urban Student Missions at the North American Mission Board and also as the executive director of ReachLife Ministries, the nonprofit ministry of Reach Records. For nearly six years, he pastored a congregation in Kansas City. D. A. earned his bachelor degree in biblical studies at Calvary Bible College and his master's in Christian studies from Calvary Theological Seminary, and he is currently working on a PhD in applied theology from Southeastern Baptist Theological Seminary. He and his wife, Elicia, have three precious children.

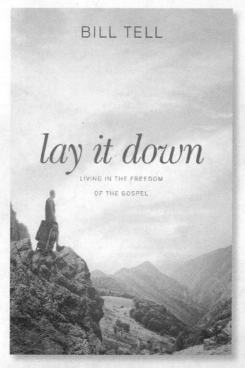

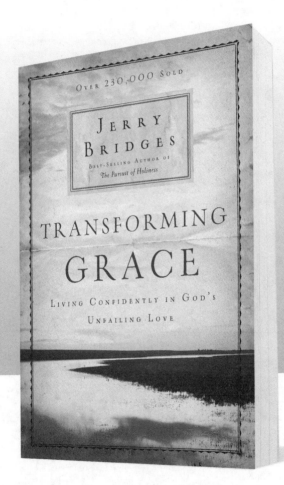